LANGUAGE IN
POPULAR FICTION

Language in Popular Fiction is a very readable, illuminating, and often hilariously funny look at the way language is put to use in thrillers and in romantic fiction. It examines its subject at three interrelated levels: a level of verbal organization, a level of narrative structure, and a level at which stylistic options and devices are related to notions of gender.

We are introduced to 'the protocol of pulchritude: a vision of woman from the waist upwards, based on perfect symmetry of feature', and to 'her symmetrical mate, he whose hairline cannot recede'. These investigations are playful, often parodic, but are firmly based on stylistic or linguistic analysis of a wide range of 'popfiction' and 'magfiction' – sources referred to include:

Barbara Cartland: *The Naked Battle*
Raymond Chandler: *Farewell, My Lovely*
Catherine Cookson: *Tilly Trotter*
Frederick Forsyth: *The Day of the Jackal*
Ian Fleming: *Live and Let Die*
Victoria Holt: *Mistress of Mellyn*
Robert Ludlum: *The Parsifal Mosaic*
Judith Krantz: *Mistral's Daughter*
Wilbur Smith: *The Leopard Hunts in Darkness*
Jacqueline Susann: *Valley of the Dolls*

Nash's beguiling exploration of the language contained between the raised rhinestone covers informs, entertains, and above all invites serious reflection on popular fiction and its claims on the reader.

'Nash has shown how analysis of narrative technique and style can illuminate popular ("airport") fiction without inflating the experience of reading it or condescending (too much) to it. *Language in Popular Fiction* challenges academic prejudice that the writing of Forsyth, Krantz, *et al.* simply does not exist, and it suggests various ways the shrewd and critical reader can read the culture, the reader, and the text of recreational fiction.'
                              Professor George Dillon, University of Washington

The Author

Walter Nash is Professor of Modern English Language at the University of Nottingham. His academic interests include English usage, composition, stylistics, rhetoric, and the language of literature, and he has published widely in these areas, including most recently *The Language of Humour: Style and Technique in Comic Discourse* (Longman, 1985), *English Usage: A Guide to First Principles* (Routledge, 1986), *Rhetoric: The Wit of Persuasion* (Blackwell, 1989), and numerous articles. He has also written a comic novel, *Kettle of Roses* (Hutchinson, 1982).

The INTERFACE Series

'A linguist deaf to the poetic function of language and a literary scholar indifferent to linguistic problems and unconversant with linguistic methods, are equally flagrant anachronisms.' – Roman Jakobson

This statement, made over twenty-five years ago, is no less relevant today, and 'flagrant anachronisms' still abound. The aim of the INTERFACE series is to examine topics at the 'interface' of language studies and literary criticism and in so doing to build bridges between these traditionally divided disciplines.

The Series Editor

Ronald Carter is Senior Lecturer in English Studies and Director of the Centre for English Language Education at the University of Nottingham. He is also Chair of the Poetics and Linguistics Association (PALA) and National Language Training Advisor for the DES (Department of Education and Science).

Titles already published in the INTERFACE series include:

David Birch: *Language, Literature and Critical Practice – Ways of analysing text*
Alan Durant and Nigel Fabb: *Literary Studies in Action*
Michael Toolan: *Narrative – A critical linguistic introduction*

LANGUAGE IN POPULAR FICTION

WALTER NASH

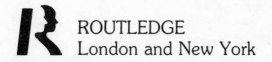

ROUTLEDGE
London and New York

First published 1990
by Routledge
11 New Fetter Lane, London EC4P 4EE

Simultaneously published in the USA and Canada
by Routledge
a division of Routledge, Chapman and Hall, Inc.
29 West 35th Street, New York, NY 10001

Phototypeset in Linotron Souvenir 10/11pt by
Input Typesetting Ltd, London
Printed in the British Isles by
The Guernsey Press Co. Ltd, Channel Islands

British Library Cataloguing in Publication Data

Nash, Walter
  Language in popular fiction. – (Interface).
  1. Fiction in English, 1945–. Style
  I. Title II. Series
  823'.914'09

Library of Congress Cataloging-in-Publication Data

Nash, Walter.
    Language in popular fiction/Walter Nash.
      p.   cm. – (Interface series)
    Bibliography: p.
    Includes index.
    1. English fiction—20th century—History and criticism.
  2. American fiction—20th century—History and criticism.
  3. Popular literature—Great Britain—History and criticism.
  4. Popular literature—United States—History and criticism.
  5. English language—Style. I. Title. II. Series: Interface
  (London, England)
  PR888.P68N37 1990
  823'.9109—dc20   89–10464

ISBN 0–415–04047–7
ISBN 0–415–02944–9 pbk

Contents

vi Contents

5 Standard ingredients: faces, places, fights,

Series editor's introduction to the Interface series

There have been many books published this century which have been devoted to the interface of language and literary studies. This is the first *series* of books devoted to this area commissioned by a major international publisher; it is the first time a *group* of writers have addressed themselves to issues at the interface of language and literature; and it is the first time an international professional association has worked closely with a publisher to establish such a venture. It is the purpose of this general introduction to the series to outline some of the main guiding principles underlying the books in the series.

The first principle adopted is one of not foreclosing on the many possibilities for the integration of language and literature studies. There are many ways in which the study of language and literature can be combined and many different theoretical, practical, and curricular objectives to be realized. Obviously, a close relationship with the aims and methods of descriptive linguistics will play a prominent part, so readers will encounter some detailed analysis of language in places. In keeping with a goal of much work in this field, writers will try to make their analysis sufficiently replicable for other analysts to see how they have arrived at the interpretive decisions they have reached and to allow others to reproduce their methods on the same or on other texts. But linguistic science does not have a monopoly in methodology and description any more than linguists can have sole possession of insights into language and its workings. Some contributors to this series adopt quite rigorous linguistic procedures; others proceed less rigorously but no less revealingly. All are, however, united by a belief that detailed scrutiny of the role of language in literary texts can be mutually enriching to language and literary studies.

Series of books are usually written to an overall formula or design. In the case of the Interface series this was considered to be not entirely appropriate. This is for the reasons given above, but also because, as the first series of its kind, it would be wrong to suggest that there are formulaic modes by which integration can be achieved. The fact that all the books address themselves to the integration of language and literature in any case imparts a natural and organic unity to the series. Thus, some of the books in this series will provide descriptive overviews, others will offer detailed case studies of a particular topic, others will involve single author studies, and some will be more pedagogically oriented.

This variety of design and procedure means that a wide variety of audiences is envisaged for the series as a whole, though, of course, individual books are necessarily quite specifically targeted. The general level of exposition presumes quite advanced students of language and literature. Approximately, this level covers students of English language and literature (though not exclusively English) at senior high-school/upper sixth form level to university students in their first or second year of study. Many of the books in the series are designed to be *used* by students. Some may serve as course books – these will normally contain exercises and suggestions for further work as well as glossaries and graded bibliographies which point the student towards further reading. Some books are also designed to be used by teachers for their own reading and updating, and to supplement courses; in some cases, specific questions of pedagogic theory, teaching procedure, and methodology at the interface of language and literature are addressed.

From a pedagogic point of view it is the case in many parts of the world that students focus on literary texts, especially in the mother tongue, before undertaking any formal study of the language. With this fact in mind, contributors to the series have attempted to gloss all new technical terms and to assume on the part of their readers little or no previous knowledge of linguistics or formal language studies. They see no merit in not being detailed and explicit about what they describe in the linguistic properties of texts; but they recognize that formal language study can seem forbidding if it is not properly introduced.

A further characteristic of the series is that the authors engage in a direct relationship with their readers. The overall style of writing is informal and there is above all an attempt to lighten the usual style of academic discourse. In some cases this extends to the way in which notes and guidance for further work are presented. In all cases, the style adopted by authors is judged to be that most appropriate to the mediation of their chosen subject matter.

We now come to two major points of principle which underlie the conceptual scheme for the series. One is that the term 'literature' cannot be defined in isolation from an expression of ideology. In fact, no academic study, and certainly no description of the language of texts, can be neutral and objective, for the sociocultural positioning of the analyst will mean that the description is unavoidably political. Contributors to the series recognize and, in so far as this accords with the aims of each book, attempt to explore the role of ideology at the interface of language and literature. Secondly, most writers also prefer the term 'literatures' to a singular notion of literature. Some replace 'literature' altogether with the neutral term 'text'. It is for this reason that readers will not find exclusive discussions of the literary language of canonical literary texts; instead the linguistic heterogeneity of literature and the permeation of many discourses with what is conventionally thought of as poetic or literary language will be a focus. This means that in places as much space can be devoted to examples of word play in jokes, newspaper editorials, advertisements, historical writing, or a popular thriller as to a sonnet by Shakespeare or a passage from Jane Austen. It is also important to stress how the term 'literature' itself is historically variable and how different social and cultural assumptions can condition what is regarded as literature. In this respect the role of linguistic and literary theory is vital. It is an aim of the series to be constantly alert to new developments in the description and theory of texts.

Finally, as series editor, I have to underline the partnership and co-operation of the whole enterprise of the Interface series and acknowledge the advice and assistance received at many stages from the PALA Committee and from Wendy Morris at Routledge. In turn, we are all fortunate to have the benefit of three associate editors with considerable collective depth of experience in this field in different parts of the world: Professor Roger Fowler, Professor Mary Louise Pratt, Professor Michael Halliday. In spite of their own individual orientations, I am sure that all concerned with the series would want to endorse the statement by Roman Jakobson made over twenty-five years ago but which is no less relevant today:

> A linguist deaf to the poetic function of language and a literary scholar indifferent to linguistic problems and unconversant with linguistic methods, are equally flagrant anachronisms.

In *Language in Popular Fiction* Walter Nash writes with characteristic perception about a genre of writing normally excluded from courses in literary studies, and demonstrates that within a wider definition of literary and cultural studies any such exclusion is difficult to justify. The texts examined in this book as 'women's fiction' and 'men's fiction' are popular in that they attract prodigiously large readerships and Walter Nash shows what interesting linguistic and cultural phenomena they are. He examines popular fiction at different linguistic levels from vocabulary to the larger patternings of discourse and generic organization and relates these in illuminating ways to more traditional literary concerns with theme and character. This is, however, not simply a text-immanent procedure since Walter Nash also explores popular fiction as a site for the negotiation of social meanings and for the mediation of ideologies. This contribution to the Interface series continues the genre which Professor Nash has started in the serious academic book on language and literary matters which is entertaining (and in places sidesplittingly funny) to read.

Preface

A generic study of popular fiction would exceed the limits I have set myself, and is probably beyond my capacity. This essay is the product of readings in the kinds of fiction composed with an eye on Him or Her: that is, in the main, thrillers and romances. By thus limiting the scope of the work I have perhaps denied myself full access to some important themes, and may well have presented an over-simplified account of the impact of popular fiction, its particular audiences, its inherent ideologies, its gradations of appeal. I am well aware that there is great diversity in these stories; that they are written with all sorts of motives, by all sorts of people; that some have pretensions which others do not; that they may be read by men and women alike; and that authors seeking a mass market do not penalize themselves by writing exclusively for one gender. I am, I repeat, well aware of what the subject involves, but in reducing my choice of material I have accepted the risk that some things may be omitted or passed over lightly.

My brief was, in any case, to write about style. This I have attempted to do at three levels: a level of verbal choice and organization, a level of narrative structure, and a level at which stylistic options and devices are related to the ideologies of manliness and womanliness which we either bring to our reading or derive from it. In the prevailing language of criticism 'ideology' is an important word. It does not occur very prominently or frequently in this book, though I do not think I have failed to describe the ideas and social assumptions encoded in current popular fiction. It would in fact be difficult to treat stylistic questions without some descriptive account of the ideologies inherent in the style. It seems to me, however, that the subject of ideology in popular fiction is complex and calls for a book of its own. One of the complexities is historical; ideologies change, or persist with a difference. (Thus Richard Hannay, for example, merges into James Bond.) Another kind of complexity is societal, and involves changes of ideological pitch to court the assent of different classes or social groupings. There are still other kinds, and had I taken it upon myself to examine them all, I should have written a different book, a better one, perhaps, more useful, possibly, but at all events different. It would not have been about style incidentally touched by ideology; it would have been about ideology incidentally governing style.

Because I thought it appropriate to a subject which is not, after all, the most solemn in the world, it has suited me to frame my essay playfully, and to indulge here and there in a little stylistic fun. I suppose that there may be some significance in my use of the image of flight as a sustaining narrative device; it could suggest, perhaps, a fugitive state of mind, a wish to avoid the constraints of 'academic' discussion. That, however, is not what has disconcerted some good friends who have read the book in manuscript. Their fear is that my levity may be taken for contempt and condescension. Should the book give that impression, I can only insist that I look down on no one, that I mock nobody's taste (or if I do, I mock my own), and that I certainly do not disparage popular fiction for being popular, though I reserve the right to smile at absurdities in any style, popular or otherwise. I have not treated my authors with less respect than I would show them if their names were securely lodged in the literary canon, and wherever I have attempted criticism, I have done so with close reference to particulars. My general attitude is that of Duke Theseus, whose words I have chosen as an epigraph because they apply to this study as well as to the fictions it describes.

WN
University of Nottingham

The best in this kind are but
shadows; and the worst are
no worse, if imagination
amend them.

*A Midsummer Night's
Dream*

Acknowledgements

The author and publishers gratefully acknowledge the following sources for material reproduced in this book:

The following authors for extracts from *Woman*: Sue Gee for 'Someone Remembered'; Maeve Binchy for 'Change of Heart'; Helen Forrester for 'A Matter of Friendship' (© Helen Forrester 1986, first published by *Woman* 1986)

The following authors for extracts from *My Weekly*: Levannah Lloyd for 'House of Whispers'; P.E.M. Nesbitt for 'Watch it, Mrs Ingram!'; Michelle Lee for 'Travelling Lady'; E. M. Holland for 'That Sinking Feeling'

True Story for extracts from 'Too Much Love' and 'Another Way'

Arrow Books for extract from *The Naked Battle* by Barbara Cartland

Berkley Publishing Group for extract from *License Renewed* by John Gardner

Collins Publishers for extracts from *Levkas Man* by Hammond Innes, *Night of Error* by Desmond Bagley, and *Mistress of Mellyn* by Victoria Holt

Corgi Books for extracts from *Tilly Trotter* by Catherine Cookson, *Mistral's Daughter* by Judith Krantz, and *Valley of the Dolls* by Jacqueline Susann

Curtis Brown Ltd for extract from *The Survivors* by Simon Raven

Faber and Faber Ltd and Random House for extracts from 'Air Port' and 'Footnotes to Dr Sheldon, 1' from *Collected Poems* by W. H. Auden

Robert Hale Ltd and Margaret Redfern for extracts from 'Dark Rhapsody' (first published in *Woman's Weekly*)

Robert Hale Ltd and Kathryn Stacey for extract from 'The Governess' (first published in *Woman's Weekly*)

Hamish Hamilton and Ed Victor Ltd for extracts from *Farewell, My Lovely* by Raymond Chandler

William Heinemann Ltd for extracts from *Eagle in the Sky* and *The Leopard Hunts in Darkness* by Wilbur Smith

Hodder & Stoughton for extracts from *King Rat* by James Clavell

Mills & Boon Publishers for extracts from *Summer's Awakening* and *Bed of Roses* by Anne Weale; *Escape to Love* by Claudia Jameson; and *Marina's Sister* by Barbara Perkins

Henry Morrison Inc. and Grafton Books for extract from *The Parsifal Mosaic* by Robert Ludlum

Pan Books for extracts from *34 East* by Alfred Coppell, *Live and Let Die* and *Diamonds are Forever* by Ian Fleming, and *The Poseidon Adventure* by Paul Gallico

Penguin Books for extract from *Cold Comfort Farm* by Stella Gibbons

Transworld Publishers for extracts from *The Day of the Jackal* and *The Devil's Alternative* by Frederick Forsyth

The author and publishers have made every effort to obtain permission to reproduce copyright material throughout this book. If any proper acknowledgement has not been made, or permission not received, we would invite any copyright holder to inform us of this oversight.

1 Prelude: in the airport lounge

But here we are nowhere, unrelated to day or our mother
   Earth in love or in hate; our occupation
Leaves no trace on this place or each other who do not
   Meet in its mere enclosure but are exposed
As object for speculation . . .
                    (W. H. Auden, *Air Port*)

Viola: What country, friends, is this?
Captain: This is Illyria, lady.
                  (Shakespeare, *Twelfth Night*)

Here in the airport lounge, how becalmed we voyagers are, all spellbound and dreambound! How equable this climate – this mild, well-regulated air, untouched by frost or torrid heat, or the bite of chilling wind! Suspended between Somewhere and Elsewhere, we bask in the light of Anywhere. It is a place where fantasies luxuriate. As our feet wander the mute and carpeted acres, our eyes flit speculatively among figures and faces. Look, now, at this man coming towards us. His neat blue suit proclaims the businessman, but who knows what underworlds of espionage, what services in a secret cause are implicated in that briefcase? Those policemen at the boarding gate are tensely waiting for the two drug-trafficking mafiosi to show up. That woman's elegance, ever so slightly ruffled – for her silk scarf hangs negligently, and she has just dropped a glove – tells us that she is on her way to meet her lover, the American neurosurgeon, who will never marry her as long as his demented wife (of whom she has no knowledge) still lingers on in the expensive Swiss clinic. Here we all are, in this Land of In-Between. We are characters in enjoyably bad books, it seems. We are in the right place for Popular Fiction.

And there in the corner is the very emblem of our condition – the airport bookstall, stacked with magazines and paperbacks to keep us happy and hypnotized in our confinement. The covers are gaudy with all the emblems and personalities of the dream-world. Here a pale face framed in a nurse's cap is bedewed with one bright tear; here a lady of phenomenal endowment sustains a gown that seems about to abandon her completely; here a gentleman whose face appears to have been fashioned out of lacquered aluminium, so smooth it is and so symmetrical, holds in crossed hands a red, red rose and a big black pistol; here the *Totenkopf* and other Nazi paraphernalia – or perhaps the hammer and sickle and the insignia of the KGB – are suspended above the heroic heads of a United States naval officer and a redhead in a tight white blouse; here is a cowboy, with ten-gallon hat and leather chaps; here is a space-trekking crewman in his galactic dungarees. There is stuff here to sustain us during our flight; and when we have emerged into the weathers of our destinations and the happenings of ordinary lives, we can always leave the book of our choice in some hotel room, to beguile another traveller.

For this is one of the principal characteristics of popular fiction – its disposability. You may buy Conrad or Henry James or Fielding in paperback, but you are hardly likely to leave them intentionally in a bedroom or on a luggage rack, because they have served their turn and have nothing left to offer you. Such authors are resources on which we repeatedly draw, and when we buy one of their books we take some care to keep it by us. Popfiction, on the other hand (let us call it that for convenience' sake) has little to offer after the first absorbed reading. We do not want *again*, though we may want *more*. To one classic book we may well return times without number; our return to popfiction consists of buying more popfiction. It is well known that popfiction is marketed by the tens of thousands, whereas fiction of more elevated pretensions sells at best by the thousand and sometimes by the mere hundred. The phrase 'best seller' points to the importance of commercial success as a popular measure of value. Between the publisher and the consumer there is a tacit agreement that if a book is good it is bound to be a best seller, and if it is a best seller it is bound to be good. And as Viscount Melbourne said in quite another context, no damned merit in it.

Of course it depends what you mean by merit. Popfiction does have its merits, and they are by no means negligible. They are shown in the ability to tell a tale, to devise its episodes with such skill that the reader often cannot bear to put the book aside, to touch on common sympathies, to understand the judgements and desires of ordinary people, to offer the keen experience of danger, of anxiety, of love, of sorrow, of triumph, but all without the intruding shadow of the actual, without obliging us to quit the Illyrian trance, so to speak, or the hermetic fold of the airport lounge. To do all this takes talent, and the money we pay for our distraction is fairly earned; we are ill-natured, and doubtless ill-informed, if we despise the arts that easily divert us.

Our deeper allegiance, nevertheless, is to a very special kind of 'merit', which we detect in the capacity of a book to illuminate our own experience, to enlarge our perceptions of human nature and conduct, and, without overt moralizing, to establish and confirm in us the knowledge of a morality. The lessons of 'serious' literature are not quickly learned. Our relationship with a book, our understanding of its themes, our view of its characters, can accrue and change over a period of many years. This is why we hold on to texts we recognize as classics, or as classic in potential. Popfiction, the disposable article, is committed to the simplest moralities, the crudest psychologies, and has few philosophical pretensions. It does not ask for careful reading or repeated reading; nor do rereadings change our understanding of its nature, our perceptions of the message it has to convey; its peculiar claim on our attentions is, in fact, that it can be quickly read and almost as quickly forgotten.

And why are we so quick about it? The source of our facility can be identified in a simple term: convention. We read the conventions of popular narrative like a map, a crude map that designates a route and a few easily recognizable landmarks. All narratives employ conventions, it is true, but there are degrees of complexity, of diversity, of originality in the management of conventional elements. If the 'maps' of novels by Graham Greene or L. P. Hartley or Iris Murdoch seem to present subtler apprehensions of the terrain than anything by Ian Fleming or Frederick Forsyth or Barbara Cartland, it is not because they employ different conventions. It is rather the case that in popfiction the conventions are simplified and more or less fixed, whereas in writing of more advanced pretension the conventional game is free, diverse, endlessly modified; so that even when such writings draw on some traditional form such as the moral fable, they may still succeed in handling convention unconventionally. All this has one striking consequence: that while we cannot easily predict the ramifications of 'non-popular' narratives, popfiction is nothing if not predictable. And so we read it quickly – moving rapidly through the landscape, as it were, seeing little but the road.

The predictabilities of situation and style figure most obviously in two genres or subspecies of popfiction: the romantic story, as published in women's magazines and some widely-marketed paperbacks, and the male-orientated 'thriller', the action-packed chronicle of supermanly heroes and hyperdiabolical villains. As to the first of these two categories, there is probably no species of fiction that can be read more quickly, with greater assurance to the reader of being steered in the right direction – no missed signals – no blind roads or wrong turnings – or with less compulsion to renew acquaintance in a second reading. In general, these tales present a view of women so demeaning (though unintentionally) that it must be acceptable only in what might be called the Illyrian sense: it has to be allowed for the time being by anyone who wants to make something of the story. It is this very acceptance that creates the conditions for fast and unburdened reading; and what the reader must swallow or sanction is an idea of true womanliness, a notion of femininity.

The essence of this notion is its recognition – clever, winning, anxious, but always submissive – of its role, to make a marriage and a home. Homecoming, literal or figurative, is the magazine writer's greatest good, and the proper end of most romantic narratives. Jill finally nestles into the protective arms of Jack, her eyes full of happy tears, her head full of wallpaper patterns. She has come Home; and home is where she will henceforth remain, though that prospect lies beyond the terminus of the tale. There are of course illimitable variations on the theme that all roads lead to Home, but the variations are based on some elementary scenarios, readily compounded by a blending of types. Readers of women's magazines will possibly recognize the following sketches, fictive instances of fictional themes:

Sketch 1: Jill is a secretary/a nurse/a teacher-governess. She is dedicated to her work, attractively turned out, nourishes sound moral instincts, and knows her place. Although she resists the impulse, feeling in every fibre of her being that he is not for her, she is deeply drawn to her employer, Sebastian/Alex/Greg, a consultant surgeon/company director/eminent publisher. Yet he is so impatient and brusque with her, finding fault with her every

action and seeming to have eyes only for Gisela, a fashion
model/stage star/voluptuous portrait painter/exclusive literary
agent. Then one day, to her surprise, he invites her to his apart-
ment/estate in Berkshire/son's School Sports, and while they are
alone in the library/knot garden/refreshment marquee he tries
to kiss her. Stunned, she repulses him, thinking of Gisela . . .

Sketch 2: Jill is married to Jason, an accountant with good
prospects. Their marriage ought to be idyllic, and yet . . . why
does Jill feel so *unfulfilled*? Why are breakfast times not the care-
free, bantering, tender, laughter-filled occasions they used to be?
Why is Jason spending more and more time at work? And why
does he so often call her, when his favourite dinner is in the
oven, pleading delays at the office? One Saturday morning, as
she is rummaging through the pockets of his dinner-jacket before
sending it to the dry-cleaners, she finds a perfumed note from
someone called Chantal. It is addressed to Jason. She can only
feel that this must be a woman. Though she resists the impulse
with every fibre of her being, she at length resolves to discover
the truth and if need be confront Jason with it, even at the risk
of destroying their marriage. One night when Jason goes out to
a business appointment, she follows him from the house . . .

Sketch 3: Jill is a career woman, successful in her own right
as a designer of lingerie for the American market. She drives a
custom-built Morgan two-seater, and her dark hair falls softly
over her pale oval face. Her husband, Piers, a brilliant but mildly
crippled concert pianist, is moody and aggressive – brooding,
she guesses, over her dazzling success in the rough-and-tumble
of the garment business, comparing it with the falling attendance
at his Beethoven recitals. Things are going badly between them.
If only they could have had children it might have been different.
Again and again she begs him to discuss their situation openly
. . . but he takes refuge in stormy attacks on the keyboard,
sometimes going on deep into the night. Jill, though resisting
the impulse with every fibre of her being, feels that the time has
come for her to leave Piers. One evening, while he is hunched
over the *Diabelli Variations*, she packs a valise and slips behind
the wheel of the Morgan . . .

These stories represent three primary patterns of Homecoming. (There are more, no doubt.) In type 1, woman seeks
Home, reaching it after various adventures in misunderstand-
ing. In type 2, woman defends the integrity of Home when it
appears to be threatened by a rival, or possibly by her own

impercipience. In type 3, she herself is on the point of leaving Home. Jill seeks, Jill holds, Jill abandons. Of course type 3 Jill will not be allowed (unless the magazine is rather advanced in its editorial views) to complete her scheme of abandonment. There will always be some turning point – a chance encounter, an accident, counsel from a sad stranger, a telephone call – to bring the runagate to her senses. Like the other Jills, she is tied to Home, and Home will claim her, comfort her, and confer upon her the only identity she is capable of sustaining. Her plot, in the meantime, may allow a diversity of choices; she may decide to leave Jack/Piers because their marriage has lost its meaning, or because there is an exciting new opening for her at the Los Angeles office, or because Antoine has invited her to his villa in Cannes – where, after a perfect meal under the Mediterranean stars, he will invite her to spend the night with him and she will realize how much she loves Jack/Piers.

In each narrative type there are numberless variations of incident, which, however, always conform to the simple principles that guide us through the narrative. We accompany the heroine on her journey Home, and we move through stages of the False Perception, the Revised Perception, and the Clarifying Act. The significance of the False Perception is that Jill in some way misinterprets her relationship with Jack; she supposes that he must be indifferent to her, or that she dislikes him, or that he is so dull in comparison with stylish Jeremy. With the Revised Perception comes the happy recognition that Jack is her man, that he is attracted to her, that he is vibrantly exciting, besides being utterly honest and reliable. (Unlike Jeremy, who only wants her body.) All that is then needed is the Clarifying Act, which may be something as simple as a bunch of red roses, or something as complicated as Jill's struggles to save Jack's racehorses from the blazing stables. The management of the scheme allows for all sorts of twists and complications – there may be repeated false perceptions and revisions of perception – but this, basically, is the path we predict.

Our expectations inevitably include an image of the heroine. We will anticipate – particularly if she is involved in a Sketch 1 plot – that like all her kind, from Jane Eyre onwards, she is *upwardly mobile*, an ordinary girl about to attract the attention of a man of distinction and worldly assets. In the case of magazine fiction, this anticipation possibly reflects an assessment of the social status, the pretensions, the decent day-dreams of the readership. It is apparent, at all events, that Jill habitually looks for a man with prospects, a good provider with some standing in the community. To be fit for such a mate, she herself must be capable and talented, combining a flair for dress and domestic economy with outstanding abilities as the organizer of an office, an operating theatre, a sales division, a library. Indeed, her claims to competence and spirited independence in a man's world often create the tensions of her particular case. The Career is the arch-rival of the ultimate good, Home. The lures of Career must never be allowed to take precedence over the claims of Home, but at the same time Jill's performance in her Career must indicate a personality of some substance and capacity. Her abilities and attainments in her own sphere may equal those of her man (a kind of occupational apartheid sometimes operates) but she must not outdo him. On the whole, if Home is to have its due, the magazine heroine must be highly competent in an occupation she will be prepared to forsake at need; let her be a junior solicitor, by all means, but beware of making her an eminent counsel (even Portia retired after only one dramatically successful case); let her be a ward sister, or more probably a staff nurse, but think twice before endowing her with a fellowship and a flourishing Harley Street practice; let her run the office with indispensable efficiency, but do not give her a seat on the board. In magazine stories, and in romantic fiction generally, the woman who elevates Career above Home puts her personal happiness at risk, and can even be morally reprehensible. (The TV soap opera, *Dynasty*, offers a typical example: virtuous Krystle is dedicated to the task of making a Home for her man, the silver-haired tycoon, whereas malign Alexis, the stock 'rich bitch' of the American scene, is an unhappy, restless power-broker, incapable of stable relationships, and therefore not only in permanent exile from Home, but also a threat to the very concept.)

It follows, naturally, that this capable woman must be attractive. This is the word most frequently used to describe her physical appeal; not so often 'pretty' (suggesting immaturity, uncertainty, helplessness), or 'beautiful' (a dubious word, with occasional connotations of speciousness, falsehood, even danger), but very commonly *attractive*, meaning wholesome, well-groomed, having regular features, a trim figure, a decent complement of teeth, full red lips, and a face which may be oval, heart-shaped, high-cheekboned, 'interesting', but never round, square, or pasty. The magazine illustrations supply the protocol of pulchritude: a vision of woman from the waist upwards, based on perfect symmetry of feature. Poised symmetrically with her is her symmetrical mate, he whose hairline cannot recede, whose jaw has immaculate definition, whose ears, discreetly proportioned and tastefully whorled, lie close to his skull, whose nose runs true, whose eyebrows are well-aligned, whose tie is becomingly knotted and lies in direct descent from his Adam's apple and the roguish cleft in his chin. The hero cannot be otherwise; can we imagine a romantic tale in which the leading man is an obese plumber? A costing clerk with flat feet? A wheezing, maladroit turf accountant who is forced to hide in the stair cupboard every time the doorbell rings? Such men may be welcome in other fictional locations, but they are not *habitués* of the romantic Home.

Nor indeed is there much of a place for them in the Great Outdoors of the thriller: on the bald and perilous moor, in the sunken liner's bullion room, in the abandoned mine, on the high girders, in the smoky back office, behind the wheel of the Lamborghini, astride the stallion or the Harley Davidson, in the various locations of crisis where a man must be ready to fire the gun, throw the punch, kick away the knife, play for time, fling himself sideways, dive off the cliff. The heroes of thrillers are a versatile breed; yet, like the heroines of magazine fiction, they act under the limitation of rival principles. Jill is caught between Career and Home; Jack is held between Self and Organization. In the Self, the thriller hero enacts his reader's gross fantasies of danger and devilry, pursuing his charmed career from one violent crisis to another, leaving behind him a trail of broken bottles, cracked crowns, grateful blondes, and defunct bullies, not to mention the wreckage of much valuable property in the form of aircraft, boats, cars, houses, industrial plant, and highly secret underground germ warfare installations. But all this might bring upon him charges of unbridled criminality and gross moral turpitude, were he not under the restraint of the Organization that sanctions his excesses.

All true heroes belong to some Organization, in the name of which they act. It may be the police force, or the regiment, or the secret service, or more generally some community of people with the right stuff in them, the good guys, the democrats, the boys, Our Gang. It is, to be sure, an essential feature of the thriller that Jack must commonly act alone, complete in the stern solitude of his manhood, making tremendous decisions, facing enormous odds with his customary fortitude and ingenuity; and this he does for the day-dreaming comfort of all men who dread the dentist and go out with their wives on Saturday mornings to appraise the rival merits of washing machines. Nevertheless, Jack Hero cannot be allowed to act merely as pleasurable inclination takes him, pushing his adversary into the combine harvester for the impure joy of homicide. In his extreme manifestations he is a kind of sanctified terrorist. His violent and murderous acts must be seen as regrettable necessities, deeds committed in a larger cause, sanctioned or ordered by the Organization. A classic case is Ian Fleming's hero, James Bond, an urbane killer whose adventures in slaughter and mayhem are briefly intercalated with notes on his prowess as a Lothario and bon viveur. Bond as Bond is really a very unpleasant man; but James Bond is also Commander Bond, an officer in the Royal Navy, and Commander Bond, furthermore, is 007, a numbered agent in the Secret Service. As 007 he is responsible only to the Organization that gives him his famous 'licence to kill'. He is under orders from his overlord, M, and his travel arrangements are administered by the severe and virtuous Miss Moneypenny. M and Miss Moneypenny are the organizational tokens of Bond's ultimate respectability, the representatives of the right side, the good cause in the furtherance of which 007 risks his life and takes his pleasure. They are in a sense his family. They are indeed no more than tokens, but the briefest indication of an allegiance is enough to distinguish the worthy hero from monstrous freebooters who kill for gain, like the central figure in Frederick Forsyth's *The Day of the Jackal*. The true hero, though he may act in splendid isolation, yet acts for Britain, for the West, for the Team, against the Rival Firm which as a rule supplies his adversaries; though sometimes these may be drawn from within the Team itself, whether as plain traitors or as well-meaning but misguided people who disapprove of the hero's activities and conspire to oppose and frustrate them. The theme of the Heroic Self versus the Organization grows almost inevitably out of the parent concept of the Heroic Self *within* the Organization.

Now it is really remarkable – we reflect as we sit in the airport lounge – that we readers of popfiction should know so much about the stories we are going to read; know it before we have turned a leaf, know it more and more as the tale progresses, with increasing confidence in our ability to predict a course of events and understand a social and moral history. You may often enter the tale at random, as the book falls open, and still pick up the thread of the story within a page or two – much as you were able to make sense of last night's TV soap, although it had been running for half an hour when you switched on your set. It scarcely matters, sometimes, where you find yourself in the narrative; the characters and their predicaments will be made manifest in the episode you are reading. In this respect, the serials in women's magazines will readily accommodate you, the more especially since a helpful editorial staff will have composed an introductory résumé like the following, from *Woman's Weekly*:

When HOLLY MERRIMAN was invited to stay at Gregory's, the elegant Northumbrian home of writer ELLIE TREVONE, she gladly accepted. Her friend Sophie was the old lady's companion. Holly, who was spending a holiday thirty miles away with her parents and six-year-old sister Rose, needed some time to herself to ponder on her future as a feature writer on a sensation-seeking newspaper just outside London. At Gregory's, Ellie turned out to be a down to earth woman in her eighties, who doted on her godson, the world-acclaimed pianist GUY WILLFORD. Holly was one of his greatest fans, but meeting him in person was somewhat disappointing. He was abrupt and aloof, though by the end of her visit he had decidedly warmed towards her and she was reluctant to leave.

Their next encounter, in London, wasn't so amicable. She'd never told him she was a journalist and, when her editor sent her to interview him, his accusation that she'd betrayed both his and Ellie's trust forced her into reaching a decision about her job. After handing in her resignation, Holly didn't have time to be despondent. Sophie phoned to announce that she was getting married and later, at the wedding reception, Holly agreed to take her place as Ellie's companion. She and Guy had reached a truce and over the next few weeks she couldn't stop thinking about him. Then one June day he appeared and, when he kissed her, she realised she was in love with him. But an unexpected guest at Gregory's soon brought her down to earth. Guy returned from a concert tour with glamorous American model TANIA FRANKTON. They seemed more than just friends and one day Tania began talking about marriage. Holly was sure that Guy was the reason for that dreamy

look in the model's eyes. That was why, when Guy started to
kiss Holly passionately, she pushed him away, believing he
couldn't resist a little flirtation even though his fiancee was in
the same house! After coming back from the wedding of her
friends MARCUS and ANNA in London, however, Holly was
surprised to find that Tania had flown to the States . . . to
get married. Guy told Holly he'd merely been acting as the
American's guardian while she was in England. Stunned, Holly
revealed what she had thought about his behaviour. He was
very angry and, as she left him, she was convinced that their
friendship had ended.

This outline ushers in the final episode of a story called 'Dark
Rhapsody'. Stylistically it takes on some of the reportorial
characteristics of tabloid journalism, notably in its designations
of the people-about-the-plot: 'writer Ellie Trevone', 'world-
acclaimed pianist Guy Wilford', 'glamorous American model
Tania Frankton'. It packages for us everything we need to know
about Holly's progress towards Home. Here are the attributes –
as 'a feature writer on a sensation-seeking newspaper' – estab-
lishing competence in the Career she will be able to relinquish
without regret. Here are Guy's credentials: he is a 'world-
acclaimed pianist', a man obviously worth sacrificing her Career
for. (The illustration confirms this; he has the obligatory chiselled
and laundered look.) Here are the familiar accessory agents –
the wise older woman, the glamorous distraction, the appealing
moppet ('six-year-old sister Rose'). Above all, here is an account
of False and Revised Perceptions, requiring only the complement of the Clarifying Act. We are dull readers indeed if we
cannot predict how in the concluding episode wise old Ellie will
explain things, and little Rose, by naughtily getting lost, will
precipitate the Clarifying Act (that search on the defective bicycle
in the pouring rain) which will bring the lovers more or less
together until final explanations from Guy lead to the ultimate
declaration of Homecoming:

> His arms went round her, gathering her close to him until they
> were lost in each other, oblivious to the world. Perhaps, Holly
> reflected dreamily, Justin Willford was right. Sometimes there
> was no need for words.

She rejects her Career as a feature-writing journalist, renounces
her plans to write a book, puts 'words' aside in order to enter

Home. And this is so readily predictable that given the characters alone, with their names, their occupations, their ages, and their adjectival dossiers, we might have written the same story, deviating from the actual product only in the choice of episode and incidental detail.

Deeply involved in the predictability of magazine narrative is the sense of a moral content. The moralizing generally accrues round the narrative elements of False and Revised Perception; it has to do with not judging by appearances, with 'trying to understand', with your responsibility to others, with seeing where your duty and your happiness lie. The moral message goes step by step with the narrative structure, and is never challenged, as far as the reader is concerned, by any ambivalent or conflicting circumstance in the fable. Here, for example, is the substance of a piece of fiction called 'Too much love', published in *True Story* (a magazine containing '10 true-to-life stories', all written in the first person and quite obviously aimed at the newly-married or the would-be-married):

Angie has been married to Ian for six months. She is blissfully happy; she even gets on well with his mother, Marianne, a wise and winsome widow, who makes a friend of her daughter-in-law, bringing her counsel, pot plants, and tickets for fashion shows. Angie appreciates these attentions, regretting only that she is such a bad hand with a cyclamen; the one Marianne has given her is 'limp and yellow'. 'I would have hated Marianne to think I hadn't looked after it properly', Angie reflects, having stowed the dead plant away in the garage.

The fact is, that Angie has little time for anything apart from Ian, his clean shirts, his steak-and-kidney pie, and his altogether engrossing presence. She dismisses his kindly suggestions that she should get out more. She only wants to be with him, and insists on accompanying him everywhere, even when he goes down to the *Red Lion* to play darts with the boys. 'Only when I sat down', she confesses, 'did I notice that no-one else in either team had brought their wives'. Ian is not well pleased. His displeasure continues next morning when he has some difficulty in slipping out of the house unattended, to buy his daily paper, and so on through the day, as the activities of watching television, gardening, and simple reading (difficult, with Angie in his lap), are encumbered by an excess of wifely affections. 'You won't let me breathe!' he cries, at length. 'You're strangling me!' Angie is bewildered by his attitude, and devastated when he storms out of the house.

But now kindly Marianne returns, with another cyclamen, to replace the one in the garage, of which she observes, after a critical inspection, 'You've killed it with kindness'. For Angie, this is the moment of Revised Perception. 'Was that what I'd done to Ian's love?' she asks herself. 'The first glimmerings of understanding came to me. Marianne was watching me, a sympathetic expression on her face'. Indeed, wise Marianne understands all too well, for did she not almost make the same mistake with her only son? And now remains only the Clarifying Act, which is performed when Ian comes remorsefully home. To his delight, Angie decides to take up Marianne's offer of tickets for the fashion show, leaving him free for another round of darts at the *Red Lion*: 'He understood what I was doing – I was loosening my stranglehold of love. It wouldn't be easy, but I would try, because I loved Ian far too much to risk failure. I would succeed, so that the future ahead of us would hold nothing but happiness!'

Only a reader singularly resistant to didactic pressure could fail to see that the moral of this story is 'Don't smother your husband with love'. We are simply not allowed to take from it any other message (e.g. 'Women put you off your darts' or 'Cyclamens don't like water'). It has the structure of a moral fable or a fairy tale in the repeated episodes of unwisdom that simultaneously instruct the reader and mark the ascent to a crisis. It even has a kind of fairy godmother to work the magic release from the bonds of harmful enchantment. It has a convenient symbolic object, the cyclamen, which we are almost invited not to notice when it enters the story, but which anyone with a modest measure of literary competence is bound to remark. There are no concealed mechanisms, no hidden assumptions, no doubtful issues. Everything is plain from the beginning, and everything enforces the moral.

Now here, by way of comparison, is the story-line of another marital tale:

Frank and Marge are off to Kenya for the holiday of a lifetime – a game-shooting safari guided by a real White Hunter. Marge finds herself strangely drawn to Will, the guide, with his keen blue eyes and his forthright ways, but the thought of a liaison is far from her mind until the day when Frank behaves in a cowardly manner on a lion hunt. That night she goes to Will's tent and allows him to kiss her. Next day, however, Frank redeems himself while shooting rhino, bravely withstanding a savage charge. Bewildered and hardly knowing what she is doing, Marge picks up a rifle and shoots Frank dead. 'He *would* have left you', Will remarks, adding unkindly, 'Why didn't you poison him?' Marge has no answer, for now she is alone on her *Safari of Shame*.

Anyone who does not recognize this story under the contrivance of its disguise must wonder at its failure to meet romantic prescriptions. Arguably, it has a False Perception and a Revised Perception, but what sort of Clarifying Act is it that involves the wife shooting the husband? And is not Will a rather *irregular* character, even for a philanderer? This plot simply will not fulfil its moralizing function. Marge and Frank should have gone to Africa hoping to save their marriage, which had been going on the rocks for a long time because of Marge's headstrong temperament and Frank's quiet, self-effacing ways. When Frank *seemed* to be cowardly on the lion hunt (but he had spotted the little native child in his line of fire) she should have gone to Will's tent and submitted to his passionate kisses, while firmly refusing his invitation to share the double cot. Then, next day, at the rhino hunt, she should have found herself in the deadly danger from which a transformed Frank would have rescued her, scorning Will's professional prudence. 'Forgive me,' she should have said, coming submissively Home to Frank's embrace, 'I'll never doubt you again' – thereby completing the necessary progress from False Perception to Revised Perception to Clarifying Act to Homecoming.

But of course the story that lurks under 'Safari of Shame' is not that kind of narrative. Its real name is 'The Short Happy Life of Francis Macomber', and its author, Ernest Hemingway, had no thought of magazine *moralizing*, though doubtless he intended his work to raise possibly complex questions of *morality*. The *moralizing* of magazine fiction is not only integrated with standard plot-mechanisms (it marches with the heroine through the successive stages of her perception), but also presents a general evaluation of conduct in various kinds of human relationship. It is a 'here's how' for the thoughtful reader. It tells her how to be a wife, how to keep her man, how to behave towards friends and colleagues. What is odd about it is, that for all its apparent claims as a practical guide to the world it is in effect highly abstract, as proverbs and folk-wisdoms are abstract in their summarizing application to a huge variety of particular cases.

In contrast, the *morality* with which writers like Hemingway deal is not systematically linked with any plot-conventions, issues no 'here's how' recipes, gives no general advice about conduct. It is concrete and specific, concerning one situation only, and one set of characters; and it calls upon the reader to make judgements on matters that are so far from straightforward that they may appear in different lights at repeated readings. Such judgements, moreover, are rarely centred on one character alone. In 'Macomber' there are three characters – Francis, Margaret, and the hunter, Wilson – diversely culpable, diversely excusable, yet motivationally linked to each other. Francis Macomber finds his manhood after (though not explicitly *because*) his wife has betrayed him sexually; in betraying him, or her notion of him, she loses her hold over the man; Wilson, in cynically abetting her deed of betrayal, underwrites the act of murder that so outrages him. Much of this is in Hemingway's power to control and express in the structure and language of his story, but much becomes implicit in the story as it is told; the tale generates a moral power perhaps beyond the intentions of the teller, and thereby becomes a very concrete and specific instance of an enquiry into the springs of human conduct. Such *morality* is a rather different thing from popfictional *moralizing*.

In its simpler forms, such as the magazine story, popfiction organizes its moralizing in a fairly obvious way. The organization becomes less obtrusive as narrative sophistication advances towards a status denotable as 'literature'. To adopt a term from current linguistics, there is a *cline*, a qualitative and technical range, from the basic product to the most advanced examples. Barbara Cartland and Ian Fleming come lower down the cline than Catherine Cookson and Alastair MacLean, who perhaps do not stand quite so high as Amanda Cross and John le Carré; and authors like le Carré begin to invite the sort of scrupulous critical evaluation we habitually reserve for the canonical texts of the academic curriculum. In le Carré's writings, certainly, the easy operations of moralizing yield to a dogged wrestling with the morality of specific situations; and the situations themselves imply social and political assumptions that invite our continual questioning.

This grading and diffusion of the moralizing process – simple, certain, and explicit at the 'lower' end of the cline, complex and ambivalent at the 'higher' stages – is matched by gradations of stylistic convention. In the simpler fictions, the textual disposition of basic narrative modes, such as description and dialogue – the when and why of their occurrence – is clearly established. Furthermore, the structural management of these modes is well marked; dialogues, for example, carry (in addition to the bare reportage of utterances) various indications, such as tags and authorial comments, marking the process of the interaction from beginning to middle to end. The signs of textual structure and the conventions governing the interior management of various textual subtypes in fact appear at all stages of the stylistic cline, but are used more skilfully, more deceptively or unpredictably, and with greater variety in the more advanced forms.

What unites the most basic and the most advanced in pop-fiction, however, is an evident concept of style as something *applied* to the work. Texts are, as it were, *styled*. For the pop-fiction writer generally, style is something with local energy, shaping or decorating a particular piece of narrative. Rarely, it seems, is style conceived as a property of the text in its total structure, and therefore as a kind of ethical instrument. Thus in 'thriller' fictions, descriptions of people, places, or events are often *strenuous* in their use of language, yet lacking in a wider significance, an organic *strength*. Here, for example, is a passage from Desmond Bagley's *Night of Error*, describing the approach to the island of Tahiti and the port of Papeete:

As *Esmerelda* drew nearer to Tahiti the sea gave place to mountains, hazy green, and then we began to see the surf breaking on the beaches as we sailed along the coast. We all turned our thoughts to cold beer ashore.

Papeete, the Pearl of the Pacific, is a pleasant town with all the usual offices – banks, a hospital, shops and so forth, but it is also a collection of tin huts set down on a tropical island and therefore a trifle squalid; but the setting is magnificent. Arriving there we tied up almost in the main street and there are not many ports in the world where you can do that. Looking over the harbour you can see the island of Moorea nine miles away, a volcano which exploded in the far past

leaving a jumble of spires and peaks leaning at impossible
angles, one of the most splendid sights in the world, and one
which must go a long way to compensate for any incon-
veniences occasioned by living in Papeete.

I looked around the harbour for the *Eastern Sun* but there
was no sign of her, so I tried to relax as we waited for customs
clearance. Campbell was fretful, anxious to go ashore and see
if there was anything for him at the post office. He was too
much in the dark concerning the Suez–Navarro expedition. I
wasn't any too patient myself. I had questions to ask and I
wanted to see the Governor. I believe in starting at the top.

As the third paragraph may suggest, there is a story to be
pushed along as briskly as possible, and the author has relatively
little time for landscape or seascape, for reflection, for word-
painting and 'atmosphere'. Story-construction, however,
requires a brief passage of description to mark the transition
between one narrative position and the next. Here accordingly,
in the first two paragraphs, is a rather distracted, patchy mingling
of descriptive devices: the ordered perspective ('the sea gave
place to mountains . . . and then we began to see the surf
breaking on the beaches'); the Baedeker note ('a pleasant town
with all the usual offices'); the hint of a picturesque phrase ('a
jumble of spires'); the conventionally emphatic adjective ('magnificent', 'squalid', 'splendid'). Collectively, these devices represent an effort to speak impressively about Papeete, so that the
reader will become aware (if it were not already apparent) that
the adventurers are moving in scenery appropriate to adventure.
Apart from this decorative striving, however, the description of
Papeete has no functional significance in the narrative.

For contrast, consider Joseph Conrad's description of a Pacific
Island at the beginning of his story *A Smile of Fortune*:

Ever since the sun rose I had been looking ahead. The ship
glided gently in smooth water. After a sixty days' passage I
was anxious to make my landfall, a fertile and beautiful island
of the tropics. The more enthusiastic of its inhabitants delight
in describing it as the 'Pearl of the Ocean'. It's a good name.
A pearl distilling much sweetness on the world.

This is only a way of telling you that first-rate sugar-cane is
grown there. All the population of the Pearl lives for it and
by it. Sugar is their daily bread, as it were. And I was coming

to them for a cargo of sugar in the hope of the crop having been good and of the freights being high.

Mr Barnes, my chief mate, made out the land first; and very soon I became entranced by this blue, pinnacled apparition, almost transparent against the light of the sky, a mere emanation, the astral body of an island risen to greet me from afar. It is a rare phenomenon, such a sight of the Pearl at sixty miles off. And I wondered half seriously whether what would meet me in that island would be as luckily exceptional as this beautiful, dreamlike vision so very few seamen have been privileged to behold.

But horrid thoughts of business interfered with my enjoyment of an accomplished passage. I was anxious for success, and I wished, too, to do justice to the flattering latitude of my owners' instructions contained in one noble phrase: 'We leave it to you to do the best you can with the ship.' . . . All the world being thus given to me for a stage, my abilities appeared to me no bigger than a pinhead.

In content this passage is generally comparable with the extract from *Night of Error*; in each case there is a ship, a tropical island, and business in prospect. One important difference, which in fairness must be noted, is that Conrad is here *beginning* a story, whereas Mr Bagley is hurrying along in mid-narrative. This in itself might well account for the relaxed, reflective impression that Conrad's paragraphs succeed in conveying. The extract is not so very much longer than its counterpart – a mere 34 words – and yet while Bagley's narrator suggests the nervous volubility of a tourist guide, Conrad's is unhurried, even amused in a wry, self-conscious way. One might of course expect a descriptive opening to be more leisurely, more ruminative, less briskly paced than a passage of transitional description. There are, however, reasons other than this for Conrad's apparently restrained tempo. Among these the most important is that whereas Mr Bagley's description skips impressionistically from one topic to another, yielding to the random impulses of 'realism' ('We all turned our thoughts to cold beer ashore'), Conrad's opening follows a programme, a symbolic programme, the iconography systematically reflecting the argument: the physical approach to the island is linked with the psychological approach to business. The link is methodically established, and so effectively as to allow an attentive reader to predict that the young captain's

fortunes in this beautiful island may be going to belie his hopes.
(If we were at all in danger of missing the connection between
the island's beauty and its commercial promise, the narrator's
own laconic commentary would remind us of it: 'This is only a
way of telling you that first-rate sugar-cane is grown there.') Thus
from the outset the description is something far more significant
than a decorative enhancement to the narrative; it is fused with
the story, essential to its development, and a necessary agent –
as the hindsighted reader must acknowledge – of Conrad's ironic
purpose.

A feeling for style as an inherent value, rather than as incidental ornament, emerges from the contrast of two ostensibly equivalent passages. The first, from Bagley:

> Looking over the harbour you can see the island of Moorea
> nine miles away, a volcano which exploded in the far past
> leaving a jumble of spires and peaks leaning at impossible
> angles, one of the most splendid sights in the world, and one
> which must go a long way to compensate for any incon-
> veniences occasioned by living in Papeete.

And the second, from Conrad:

> Mr Barnes, my chief mate, made out the land first; and very
> soon I became entranced by this blue, pinnacled apparition,
> almost transparent against the light of the sky, a mere ema-
> nation, the astral body of an island risen to greet me from
> afar. It is a rare phenomenon, such a sight of the Pearl at sixty
> miles off. And I wondered half seriously whether what would
> meet me in that island would be as luckily exceptional as this
> beautiful, dreamlike vision so very few seamen have been
> privileged to behold.

Each of these extracts concerns a striking view, a 'sight': 'one
of the most splendid sights in the world', and 'a rare phenomenon, such a sight of the Pearl'. The passages are thus superficially comparable, but in stylistic intention they are diverse. A
phrase such as Mr Bagley's '*jumble* of spires and peaks leaning
at *impossible* angles' (my italics) suggests a struggle to enforce
the description, a grabbing at lexical resources that is in fact
quite common in popfiction. Conrad's language suggests, by
contrast, that his description is imaginatively *conceived*, and that
its words are designating patterns of meaning that lie beneath
the descriptive surface. There is, for example, a lexical sequence

of abstractions − 'apparition', 'emanation', 'phenomenon', 'vision' − all suggesting ghostliness, unreality, lack of substance. And here the narrator drops a hint to the reader. He 'half seriously' wonders whether what he is about to experience will be as 'luckily' exceptional as his first haunting vision of the place. The adverbs give us oblique instructions: we are in fact to take seriously the spectral monition, and we are to understand, correspondingly, that the captain's 'luck' will indeed be 'exceptional', though perhaps not in the way he anticipates. Such instructions may of course elude us at the first reading; perhaps not until we have finished the story will we begin to comprehend the ironic shiftiness of Conrad's vocabulary when he uses such words as 'smile', 'fortune', 'pearl', and 'sweetness'. But a second reading will reveal how all the clues are there, in due place. Conrad's 'apparition' and 'emanation' are abstractions of a different order from Mr Bagley's 'jumble'. They are not simply attempts to put something forcefully. They are germane to the symbolism of the narrative. They suggest phantoms; and phantoms are deceptive; and deceit of one kind or another, deceit tending to corruption, is the very substance of Conrad's tale. That substance is reflected in the style of every page and passage in the narrative. His descriptive technique involves a continual attempt to *organize* the pervading matter of the story.

But here in the airport lounge, in this lapse of time, this bemused interval between the scenes and acts we call real, we are hardly interested in the organic style, in the words that form the patterns that truly configure and embody the nature of the tale. You brought a 'good' novel in your hand-luggage, but you are not going to read it, not here. It will be too laborious, too exacting, perhaps a little too painful; and we are here to be soothed by devices that may vividly enforce the illusion of acting, thinking, and perceiving, but will rarely oblige us to interpret the act, criticize the thought, or question the perception. We are not here to ask questions, we are here to be diverted. Go to the bookstall, then. Buy yourself a couple of magazines − and while you are at it, fetch me a thriller, some tale of adventure with pistol shots and mineral rights and a spot of intermittent hanky-panky with an amazingly available blonde. I shall need something to fend off boredom while we fly over the North Pole.

2 Woman's place: a dip into the magazines

> Man's love is of man's life a thing apart,
> 'Tis woman's whole existence.
>
> (Lord Byron)

Up, up, up. Will the climb *never* come to an end? We are rising – we are rising – we are levelling off at our cruising height – and now the little bells ring and the warning lights go out – and you can let go of my hand – and I can unclench my teeth – and while we await the jocund arrival of what in airlinespeak is called a *beverage*, we can observe our fellow passengers and see how well they have survived the ordeal. See, they are lighting votive cigarettes along there in the 'Smoking' section, and the line for the toilets is forming already – we are truly airborne. Our companion, world-famous Professor Pangloss, has all this while been engrossed in his reading, and it should not surprise you, madam, that your *Woman's Weekly* has somehow fallen into his hands. Not only is he an eager reader of these stories; rumour has it that he actually *writes* quite a lot of them – under an assumed name, of course – as an occasional diversion from his learned contributions to the *Quarterly Journal of Applied Euphorics*. In women's magazines he finds a comfortable receptivity to a philosophy which he has slightly revised since the time of his notorious acquaintanceship with young Candide. No longer prepared to assert that 'all is for the best in the best of all possible worlds', he believes none the less that 'it will all come out right in the end'.

Our professor is well aware that women's magazine fiction is composed under certain constraints, social as well as linguistic. A sort of censorship operates, a conspiracy of inclusions and deletions, the parties to which are the author, the editor, and the reading public. The author knows what the editor likes, the editor says what the public wants, the public craves what the author gives, the author writes what the editor needs . . . Thus the censorship develops. But if 'censorship' seems too harsh a word, too dictatorial in its implications, let us put it a little Panglossily and say that there is a careful *grooming of assumptions*, the purport of which is ideological. This is to use *ideology* in a sense corresponding to one of the *OED*'s definitions: 'A system of ideas concerning phenomena, especially those of social life; the manner of thinking characteristic of a class or an individual.' To fit the tendency of magazine fiction, however, the dictionary definition needs to be modified a little; editorial concern, we may think, is to promote 'a manner of thinking *considered appropriate to a class*'.

There is indeed a 'manner of thinking' that informs the magazine story, and it is almost easier to define negatively than positively. No story ever suggests that life is devoid of purpose or meaning, that destinies are random, that human beings are capriciously swayed by forces they can neither understand nor control, that at the heart of their relationships is the pathos, the despair, of realizing that one person can never 'know' another, that lovers must always be untrue, that the bridegroom at length turns away from the bride. Everything is 'meant'; things are 'meant to happen', people are 'meant for each other'. There are no existentialists in this winsome world; the life-style forbids them. There is no poverty, though there may be people who are finding it hard to make ends meet – saving up to buy their dream house, or balancing the cost of a new car against the expense of that coveted trip to the States. There is little vice or cruelty; people make redeemable mistakes, though hurtful things are sometimes said and eyes intermittently brim with stinging tears. There is no evil much beyond malice, bitchery, and the occasional machinations of stereotypical wrong'uns. There is always optimism, smiling timorously through passing clouds of bearable troubles, beaming triumphantly on the happy ending of the tale. The foundation of this optimism is confidence in the institutions of our society, the politics and beliefs that sustain the marriage, the family, and the ethos of the Home.

This entails a pervading view of woman's role in society, her place in human relationships, and the aspirations that may be regarded as legitimate and desirable. There is one story in which such a view is picturesquely articulated:

She had to be like the seaweeds she saw as she peered down from the boat, swaying forever delicately under water, with all their delicate fibrils put tenderly out upon the flood, sensitive, utterly sensitive and receptive within the shadowy sea, and never, never rising and looking forth from the water until they died, only then washing, corpses, upon the surface. But while they lived, always submerged, always beneath the wave. Beneath the wave they might have powerful roots, stronger than iron; they might be tenacious and dangerous in their soft waving within the flood. Beneath the water they might be stronger, more indestructible than resistant oak trees are on land. But it was always under-water, always under-water. And she, being a woman, must be like that.

But this is no magazine story. The writer is D. H. Lawrence, towards the end of his novella *The Fox*, in one of those passages of heavy-breathing homiletic that betray a reluctance to let the tale make its own point, and a horrid willingness to nag the reader into a state of perceptual grace. What Lawrence here prods us into perceiving is as sentimental and tendentious as anything in magazine narrative. It may be more stylishly said, but it insists, nevertheless – 'And she, being a woman, must be like that' – on the doctrine that Jill's peace is in Jack's interest. Her business is to think always of love – not as a kind of action which she initiates ('He would not have the love which exerted itself towards him', says Lawrence, adding diagnostically 'It made his brow go black'), but as a receptive state of being, greatly to be desired, the source of all power and identity. The magazine stories leave us to infer what Lawrence comes close to stating explicitly, that in her state of submersion and submission woman is somehow *more powerful* than her partner, and consequently has the last tender laugh, not only on him but also on all females who unfemininely try to *exert* themselves in love.

Elements of the story, 1: dilation

This ideological view of domestic woman, obedient and triumphant, governs the broad patterning of the stories and ultimately controls the detail of recurrent stylistic devices. In constructing their narratives, the authors habitually make use of three interlinked elements. One of these is *Relation*, that is, the description of the characters, their actions, and the events in which they are progressively involved; a second is *Dialogue*; and the third, for which it is necessary to invent a special term, is

Dilation. The word 'dilation' punningly connects 'relation' and 'dialogue', and there is indeed a useful significance in this accidental piece of word-play. What is principally meant by Dilation, however, is a widening of the field of narrative unaccompanied by an onward movement of the plot – as when the author or the narrator-within-the-tale 'dilates' on matters complementary to the story. Such matters are presented in a temporal and/or a modal perspective; that is to say, they belong to a time preceding the narrative or the current phase of action, and are thus narrated in résumé fashion, or they are speculations on unreal events. Passages composed in this mode very frequently include verbs of cognition and inert perception, such as 'think', 'know', 'remember', 'recall', 'ask oneself', 'wonder', 'concentrate', 'believe', 'sense', 'feel'; an obvious mark of the 'time-before' résumé is the past perfective tense form (e.g. 'They had met at a party'); musings on the possible and the eventual are characterized by modal verbs like 'would', 'could', 'must', 'might', and by 'reflexive' questions of the type 'Why had she come here?', 'What would Paul think?' The linguistic features that typify Free Indirect Speech are thus drawn into the stylistic texture of Dilation.

Now here are some examples of the 'dilative' style, taken from two stories in *Woman's Weekly*:

A. She had known, but momentarily forgotten, that another son did exist. Emily had told her about him. He had left Cranmere under a cloud, sent packing by his father. The nature of his offence was unknown. Neither she nor Emily had expected him to reappear so soon after the Marquess' death, if ever. He had been what was known as "a bad lot".

B. Her mind was concentrated on Conway's startling announcement and its possible repercussions. It could be – she certainly hoped so – that the new Lord Cranmere's arrival would be a good thing for the house and everyone in it.

A misspent youth didn't necessarily mean he must be a dissolute adult. He might have reformed and become quite respectable and staid. Yet if that were the case, why had he never come home? Never made any effort to repair the breach with his family?

The important question was: what would be his attitude to Emily? Would he be kind and protective? She would be

appallingly vulnerable if it turned out that the newly arrived
Marquess was still the "bad lot" he had been in his salad days.

C. Vicky was still wondering exactly what had upset Charly,
but she could see that her teenage dignity wouldn't stand for
probing. In any case it wasn't her job to get over-involved. It
was one of the pitfalls of nursing children. It had been hard
enough to stay within the bounds of professional concern
while nursing twenty children at once in the big hospital where
she had worked before, so obviously it was harder in the
one-to-one situation operated by the clinic. Simon would be
perfectly entitled to give her a dressing-down if she started
sounding over-possessive about any patient.
    She had heard him being coldly caustic to one of the nurses
for "leaping to conclusions", and had felt a startled quiver at
the icy authority in his voice which had made everyone within
hearing almost jump to attention. It had shown Vicky yet
another side to him from the man who was gentle and reassuring with a sick child, humorous yet firm with an over-confident
convalescent.

In none of these extracts is there anything that could be construed as 'action', as a contribution to the currently developing
plot. Their purpose is not so much to 'tell' the story as to 'fill
out' the story; background information is supplied, and there is
some speculation on the might-have-been and the what-could-
happen. Characteristically, these recollections attract verbs of
cognition and perception: 'know', 'forget', 'expect' in A, 'concentrate', 'hope', 'mean' in B, 'wonder', 'hear', 'feel' in C. In
passage A, the perspective is exclusively temporal, with five
instances of the past perfective in six sentences: 'She had known
. . . that another son did exist', 'Emily had told her', 'He had left
Cranmere', 'Neither she nor Emily had expected him to
reappear', 'He had been . . . "a bad lot" '. Extracts B and C are
a little more complex, diversely mingling the temporal backshift
of 'had' with the modalities of 'would' and 'could'. One notable
difference between them is that C looks to the past, whereas B
anticipates the future. Extract C labours to convey information
about the heroine's previous professional experience:

It had been hard enough to stay within the bounds of professional concern while nursing twenty children at once in the

big hospital where she had worked before, so obviously it was harder in the one-to-one situation operated by the clinic.

Passage B uses modal verbs and the question device, in speculations that look forward to future developments:

> It could be . . . that the new Lord Cranmere's arrival would be a good thing . . . The important question was: what would be his attitude to Emily? Would he be kind and protective? She would be appallingly vulnerable if it turned out that the . . . Marquess was still the "bad lot" he had been . . .

These instances show how short interludes of dilative writing can promote the illusion of retrospect and prospect; they give the story some sort of orientation in time, some sort of location in the flux of the actual and the potential.

Though such dilative episodes add nothing to the current plot, it is quite possible for a dilation to embody a little narrative, as in the following example:

> It had been so different three years ago, the night she'd met Stefan de Vaux. There'd been a party. Bella always threw a party when she'd sold a picture because poverty, she'd explained, was a great inspiration. She'd been wearing a brilliant blue caftan, her fair hair twisted on the top of her head, the severity of it accenting her high cheekbones, the little jade Buddha gleaming on its silver chain round her neck.
>
> Claire, pale from England and the illness that had allowed her to come to Tangier to recuperate, had been passed from guest to guest – "Ah, you're Bella's cousin" – like a plate of canapes, she thought ruefully, attractive but unexciting. Until Stefan de Vaux had taken her out onto the balcony and kissed her.
>
> "Well?" he'd said softly, in his lightly accented voice, letting her go at last, and she had just stood there, staring at him, at his lean, outrageously handsome face, his laughing mouth, amber brown eyes. "Angry? Pleased? Shocked?" And she'd blushed furiously, feeling all three.

The main purpose of this passage is evidently to make the backshift in narrative time that enables the author to suggest – in this particular case – a romantic history; Stefan de Vaux is the man out of the past who is perturbing the present. But there is a little story within the story here; the Dilation contains a Relation, couched in the standard style of magazine narrative, with its layers of participle clauses (see the last sentence of the first paragraph and the first sentence of the third), its little tinsel-clusters of modifiers ('a brilliant blue caftan', 'his lean, outrageously handsome face'), its obligatory spangling of manner adverbs ('ruefully', 'softly', 'furiously'). Dilation in this case involves something more than simple résumé. It serves the fuller purposes of 'flashback', recounting the action-before-the-action as well as supplying information about circumstances.

Now this strategy of recalling how things were and what happened *then* is of course not a peculiar property of women's magazine fiction. We can find versions of it in many narratives, of diverse sorts; for example, in Hemingway:

> The people he knew now were all much more comfortable when he did not work. Africa was where he had been happiest in the good time of his life, so he had come out here to start again. They had made this safari with the minimum of comfort. There was no hardship; but there was no luxury and he had thought that he could get back into training that way. That in some way he could work the fat off his soul the way a fighter went into the mountains to work and train in order to work the fat off his body.

But in *The Snows of Kilimanjaro*, from which this is taken, the function of recall and the intercutting of present and past time are so important that the narrative requires the regular counterpoise of Relation and Dilation. It is obviously part of Hemingway's plan for this particular story, not necessarily to be repeated in the same way elsewhere. Indeed, what strikes the reader about some of his shorter narratives is the deliberate avoidance of a dilative accompaniment to the bare Relation; an avoidance that makes the stories enigmatic, and leaves to the reader the task of discerning explanatory propositions and drawing moral conclusions. Some of his short stories are more laconic in this respect than others. It is a question of what each narrative requires for its own effectiveness; it is not always necessary or desirable to dilate the telling. But in a woman's magazine story, the Dilation is a conventional and almost obligatory element, and this for three reasons: first, it is the easiest way to give the reader the background to the story, when limited space, or possibly lack of skill, prevents the gradual, allusive communication of supplementary detail through dialogue; second, because it has its own 'dialogic' value, principally in representing the heroine's communings with herself; and third, perhaps the most important reason, because it is a repository for moral comment.

The moralizing mentioned in Chapter 1 as a necessary component of magazine fiction is very often contained in the dilative episodes that set the story, supply some of its transitions, and not infrequently adorn its happy endings:

> Fern could not imagine a more ill-assorted trio of friends. Yet she sensed that they would, indeed, be friends for a long time to come.

(Note the cognitive verbs 'imagine' and 'sense', and the modals 'could' and 'would'.)

> I squeezed Mum's arm, glad that she understood at least some of my feelings. I knew that my going away still hurt her, but she wanted me to have my chances, because deep down she wished she had broken away and seen a bit more of life before she settled down. Luckily for me, I realised what I wanted before it was too late . . .

(The tell-tale signs here are the verbs of cognition – 'understand', 'know', 'realise' – and volition – 'want', 'wish'.)

> Mike's smile was one of achievement, and she smiled admiringly back at him. She also made a resolution. In future she'd leave the small home repairs to him.
>
> Never again would she tell him she could manage as well as he could – even though, if the truth be told, she probably could.

(In this story from *My Weekly*, entitled 'That Sinking Feeling', a woman restores her husband's fallen self-confidence by encouraging him to unblock the sink – no doubt on the principle that a little accomplishment goes a long way. 'Would' and 'could' are the characteristic tokens of her self-communing, as she draws her moral).

> I thought of Harry, dear understanding Harry, who would be so pleased that this had happened. We still had many problems to face, but face them we would – as a family! Through foolishness and lack of understanding I had nearly lost my daughter. Thank heaven I had realised the truth in time!

(This is the ending of a narrative in *My Story*, called 'He was kind to me'. It tells mothers how to react when their teenage daughters are made pregnant by kindly strangers. Note the familiar dilative tokens, of tense – 'pleased that this had happened', 'I had nearly lost my daughter', 'I had realised the truth in time'; of modality – 'would be so pleased', 'face them we would'; and of the cognitive vocabulary – 'think', 'understand', 'realise').

As these examples may suggest, the *action* of a woman's magazine story is frequently nothing more vigorous than a change in the heroine's mental state, as she comes to perceive, understand, and believe. Her role is thus essentially passive. She must be, as Lawrence puts it, 'like the seaweeds . . . utterly sensitive and receptive . . . never rising and looking forth from the water'. Sensitivity and receptiveness, however, are in themselves no makers of narrative. The magazine writer is obliged to contrive an action – or rather, a series of small *activities*, curiously emphasized, like opening a door, lifting a cup, putting on a coat, walking across a room – to make the heroine seem to be committed to a strenuous, busy, wholly meaningful engagement with life. The illusion of *busy living* is assiduously promoted, not only in the element of Relation, but also through the structure of Dialogue.

Elements of the story, 2: dialogue

Dialogues are indispensable to magazine tales, the readers of which would certainly echo Alice's question, 'what is the use of a book without pictures or conversations?' It is seemingly a rule of composition, at the opening of a story, to get into Dialogue as quickly as possible. Here, for example, is the opening of a story summarized in Chapter 1 (p. 12), called 'Too much love':

> Marianne, Ian's mother, arrived just as I was pressing Ian's suit.
>
> "Hallo, Angie," she said, noting the jacket draped over the ironing board. "Are you two going somewhere special?"
>
> "No, I just like Ian's clothes to look nice, that's all," I replied.
>
> She chuckled. "Well, he didn't get attention like that when he lived at home, I can tell you! And what's that I can smell in the oven? Something delicious. You spoil that lad rotten, do you know that?
>
> I grinned back. "Yes, and it's fun."

I liked Marianne very much. She'd turned out to be a great mother-in-law.

"You'll have trouble there," people had warned me when I had married Ian. "A widow with an only son! She'll never let go! She'll make your life a misery!"

But Marianne hadn't been like that. In the six months that we had been married, I could honestly say that she had never interfered once. In fact, although we saw her regularly, she rarely called without being invited. Today's visit was unusual.

This introduction uses the three elements of Relation, Dialogue, and Dilation. They overlap and succeed each other in a way that makes this little passage a simple paradigm of magazine story structure. Relation is a minor, relatively trivial element, from which we learn only that Angie is pressing Ian's suit. It is immediately overtaken by Dialogue, encapsulating the information that Ian is spoiled and that Angie is cooking 'something delicious' for him. Dialogue proper extends into pseudo-Dialogue ('You'll have trouble there,' etc.), and so into Dilation (in the paragraph beginning 'But Marianne hadn't been like that'). The narrative progression is essentially that of *gossip*: 'What was she doing?', 'What was said?', 'What lay behind that?' Clearly, this story-opening follows a discursive rule. Its paradigmatic quality might be demonstrated in 'breakdown' form, thus:

Text	*Element and function*
Marianne, Ian's mother, arrived just as I was pressing Ian's suit.	Relation: identifies participants, social roles, action.
'Hallo, Angie,' she said . . . 'Yes, and it's fun.'	Dialogue: encapsulates further information about Angie's relationship with Ian.
I liked Marianne very much . . . 'You'll have trouble there,' people had warned me . . . She'll make your life a misery!'	Transitional element: a comment on the foregoing Dialogue ('I liked Marianne very much') leads into a pseudo-Dialogue – recollected speech – preparing the way – NB the past perfective, 'people had warned me' – for a passage of Dilation.

| But Marianne hadn't been like that ... Today's visit was unusual. | Dilation: necessary background information completed. |

This tabulation indicates the characteristic functioning of the three main elements of narrative structure, and also suggests a little about their overlapping or intermeshing. The common intuition that dialogue is the most prominent element in magazine fiction is not always so clearly borne out; nevertheless, the intuition is generally reliable. It reflects one of the ideological assumptions about women, that their proper sphere of action is in talk – whether as conciliators, explicators, supplicants, or simple gossips.

The dialogues of magazine fiction are in most cases *duologues*, representing exchanges of information between two persons, with no other party in attendance – though occasionally a child, a servant, a rival, will be allotted a minor role in the script. These duologues, ostensibly mimetic of everyday speech, are in many ways quite unlike naturally-occurring conversation. Superficially, they may sometimes suggest 'phatic communion', the use of language to express the sense of social bonding; but these fictional conversations are in fact designed solely to promote the narrative. They are seldom fraught with meanings indirectly expressed, or implied, or manifestly dependent on the shared knowledge of the conversationalists; if there is a meaning to be inferred, the inference is made explicit in some way, usually in a speech-reporting tag ('. . . she said, hating him'), or in an interpolated comment. They mimic the ellipses and interjections of 'ordinary' speech, but their sentences are rarely ill-formed or incomplete, seldom illogical or badly-sequenced; they present an image of discourse which is demure and tidy even when the participants are hurling reproaches at each other. In the duologue, the speakers wait their turn to agree or disagree, to exclaim, to revile, to reciprocate, to state with emphasis before turning on their heels and sweeping out of the room. What they are shown as being engaged in has little to do with 'real' conversation; the characters in the story are simply made to construct for the reader's benefit narrative patterns that would otherwise have to be worked out in continuous prose. In the matter of turn-taking, however, there is a link of sorts with naturally-occurring conversation. The fictional dialogue apes the procedure of taking turns, frequently marking the switch from one speaker to another with some small expression of an activity or a response:

> "No, I just like Ian's clothes to look nice, that's all," I replied.
> She chuckled. "Well, he didn't get attention like that when he lived at home, I can tell you!"

The sentence 'She chuckled' marks the conversational turnover, and at the same time suggests a little liveliness, an activity of sorts. Again:

> ". . . Something delicious. You spoil that lad rotten, do you know that?"
> I grinned back. "Yes, and it's fun."

Now it is 'I grinned back' that marks the exchange. These incidental snippets of commentary serve two important purposes. First, they suggest activity. Something is going on here; the two women are not merely talking to each other, they are *chuckling* and *grinning*, and the words suggest something more strenuous than mere *laughing* or *smiling*. Second, the commentary sentences are a component in the framing of the dialogue as it is scripted on the page; they are, so to speak, part of its notation. What is notated in the examples given above is a *turnover*; but commentary devices may be similarly used to mark the entry to a duologue (*turn-in*) or to indicate the exit (*turn-out*). An example of turn-out in the extract we have been considering is the statement 'I liked Marianne very much'. It is a comment on the exchanges that have just occurred; it effectively closes down that particular piece of duologue; and at the same time it creates the transition to a new phase in the narrative.

The 'turn' devices have some recurrent linguistic forms. Turn-ins are commonly short declarative sentences with the syntactic pattern SV, or SVO, or SVA, or SVC: 'The policeman smiled', 'Ed gathered his papers', 'Jill looked up in astonishment', 'Maria's face was white'. In patterns other than SVC (where of course the predicator is 'be', 'seem', 'look', 'become', etc.), the verbs denote either a specific action, like 'gather', or a facial expression – 'smile', 'frown', 'look up' – frequently implying eye-contact between the participants. Turnovers are similarly framed, but the range of verbs is a little different; they include with the verbs of facial expression denotations of response, such as 'shrug', 'flinch', 'gasp', and in some cases they imply a breaking of eye-contact (e.g. 'turn away', 'look down'). Turn-outs are variously formulated. In general, they are declarative sentences, the meaning of which necessarily indicates a suspension of the duologue: 'Jack fell silent', 'They paused at the gate', 'Jill decided she did not like Emily', 'That was where they had gone wrong, Mary reflected', might all do duty as turn-outs. A silence, a pause, a change of activity or direction, can be scripted into the duologue as turn-out markers. Verbs denoting the drawing of unspoken conclusions – e.g. 'decide', 'reflect', 'tell oneself' – are not unusual here. Turn-outs sometimes express a summarizing attitude on the part of the narrator or central character (e.g. 'I liked Marianne very much'); and the activity denoted in a turn-out may be less transient or momentary than those indicated by the verbs of the turn-in and the turnover.

The turn devices are used to frame dialogue; its constituent utterances are regularly presented with report-formulae, e.g. a verb plus a manner adverb or a participle clause. The following extract illustrates a typical construction:

Sarah looked at Katy sharply.   < turn-in

"What if he finds someone else while you're staying with your gran? What would you do then?" she asked, instantly regretting her words.   < reporting verb ('ask') + participle clause ('instantly regretting' etc.)

The girl only shrugged.   < turnover

"I don't know," she murmured thoughtfully. "I wouldn't just give up. I'd talk to him, I suppose. Find out what was missing from our relationship that made him want someone else."   < reporting verb ('murmur') + < manner adverb

"Would something have to be missing?" Sarah asked quietly, trying to hide the pain in her voice. "Couldn't it just be that he didn't love you any more?"   < verb + manner adverb + participle clause ('trying to hide' etc.)

"No ..." the girl said slowly. "At least I think I'd have noticed things before it   < verb + manner adverb

reached that stage. And I'd
have asked him straight out
what was wrong, because
that's the way I am. I'd do anything for Tony, rather than give
up on him. He's worth it."

Her gaze steady on the road
ahead, Sarah didn't answer for
a while.   < turn-out

The extract shows how the turn devices frame the duologue
(though there is often more than one turnover in a passage of
this length), and how most speeches are marked by reporting
tags. The technical devices of speech-reporting are particularly
important in women's magazine fiction, frequently making links
or overlaps between Dialogue ('what was said') and Relation
('how it was said', 'what happened while it was being said').

The grammar of reporting formulae will invite further examination. These tags have an obvious role in structuring the dialogue; what should be equally obvious is that they are often to
be read co-ordinately with the 'turn' devices, as indices to
another kind of structure, whether we regard it as a structure of
action, or feeling, or character, or perhaps more subtly as a
structuring of the reader's responses. The various kinds of verbal
tagging found in magazine fiction are arguably instructions issued
to the reader, for the stage-management of the imagination. And
if this is too large a claim, it is at all events clear that the devices
used in the presentation of dialogue may be integrated with
other narrative purposes.

Elements of the story, 3: relation

These 'other narrative purposes' comprise the element of
Relation, an element which often has to be gradually insinuated
into the pauses, the intermissions, the dilative *addenda* of dialogue. It is an oddly subordinate, 'smuggled' element in many
stories, a provision of incidents round which accretions of talk
and reflection may form. In substance it is partly static, partly
dynamic. Its static content includes:

(a) Descriptions of appearance, of dress, of faces; particularly
the latter, for the human face and its role in human interaction
– the eye-functions of looking, glancing, watching, noting, the

mouth-functions of smiling, grinning, pouting, and so forth – is a primary image in magazine fiction. The illustrations at the beginning of stories are nearly always of faces: her face, his face, their confronted faces, or a foregrounded face with a background of representative objects or scenes. In descriptions of faces and figures, the mirror is a recurrent narrator's device, whether it be the pier-glass in the boudoir or the rear-view mirror in the run-about. When the heroine is not scrutinizing other people, she demurely scrutinizes herself:

> She had been in and out of the pool all day and her bathing suit was hanging from the shower tap. Before reaching for it, she paused for a moment to look at herself in the full-length mirror. A tall girl with sun-streaked blonde hair, long brown legs and a curvy figure which she would have liked to be slimmer but which she wasn't displeased with.

Without this piece of speculation (in the literal sense of the word) we would never know what the heroine in this story looks like – *to herself*, which is the crucial consideration. It would be a stylistic error, a breach of generic convention, for the author to supply the unmediated information that Summer (the bather's name) was a good-looking lass if a bit on the plump side. Everything in a magazine story must be seen through the eyes of the central character – including the central character's own person.

(b) Descriptions of settings – houses in particular, 'backgrounds' in general; and with these, many short descriptions of matters incidental to domestic routine. A lot of attention is paid to rooms, furnishings, stairways, terraces, gardens. Brief notes on meals and casual comestibles have a peculiar importance. Ostensibly they promote the illusion of a 'real' and 'practical' sphere of action, a down-to-earth anchor for the ballooning dreams of romance that soar high above mere bacon sandwiches or steak-and-kidney pie; structurally, they may be kernel-incidents for little outgrowths of dialogue, or convenient passages of transition from one stage of the narrative to the next.

Descriptive material of this kind provides the general setting or illusionistic background of the story. ('Illusionistic' rather than 'realistic', because in apparently striving to show us the world we know and believe in, the writers succeed only in promoting an illusion of 'worldliness'. And despite its high moral tone, magazine fiction is incorrigibly worldly.)

In its more dynamic aspects, Relation consists of:

(c) Descriptions of activities, usually of a minor, instinctive, quite commonplace kind. The heroine is never called upon to dynamite the power station or kick the villain in the groin, but she *is* required to be sensitive and receptive (like the seaweed) to the minute-by-minute movement of ordinary affairs. A recurrent response is the turn-and-walk. Tennyson's description of the Lady of Shalott – 'she left the web, she left the loom, she made three paces thro' the room' – would fit the magazine heroine quite well; walking hither and thither, whether in agitation or simply to effect entrances and exits, is one of her most significant actions, along with *looking* ('regarding', 'watching', 'gazing', 'glancing', 'scrutinizing', etc.) and *responding* (with shrugs, frowns, gasps, chuckles, cheeky grins, and the like). The commonest response-action is probably the nod. 'Doing nodding' is an activity that occupies much of the time of the general personnel of magazine fiction.

(d) Descriptions of emotions and sensations: of feelings in the abstract (anger, dismay, bewilderment, uncertainty, love – a matter for apperception, this – heroines 'realize' that they are in love); and of the corporeal feel of things – of the stinging tears, of the flushing cheeks, of her resistance melting under the burning ardour of his kiss.

The relational mosaic

Descriptive material of the various types listed above is rarely introduced into magazine stories in the form of extended passages or set pieces of the sort accommodated by the narrative technique of the novel. Instead, it is cut and fitted to available places in the story, making the construction of the narrative the literary equivalent of the making of a mosaic. None of the pieces of this relational mosaic is as a rule very large; some consist of no more than a few words. They take four principal forms, definable as follows:

(a) Free-standing episodes of description, usually no more than half a dozen sentences in length, but occasionally longer, for example at the beginning of a story:

> The sky was clear, the pink-tinged horizon promising a good day. Settling herself more comfortably in her seat, Sarah concentrated on the road.
> Already, she had covered almost a third of the journey

south. Familiar sights flashed by with monotonous regularity. Sunlight, shafting through the trees, brought poignant reminders of earlier days. *Picnics in summer, country walks in spring* . . .

Her eyes softened momentarily before the anger returned. Picnics and country walks were for the past. This was the present – and every mile she drove took her further from the pain it held.

Only the future mattered now. It lay ahead, somewhere, in the alien, teeming city . . .

This opening exhibits several of the stylistic symptoms of magazine narrative. Here it will suffice to note, as a characteristic of beginnings, the dilative orientation to time (past remembered, present experienced, future anticipated), the necessary locative information (we are on the road, on a 'journey south'), and the immediate evaluation of scenes and events from the point of view of the person who is quite evidently the principal character.

(b) Shorter passages encapsulated in the course of dialogue. These somewhat resemble turnovers, but they are generally longer, and carry information over and above what may be required by the turn-device, with its customary notations of a brief response, a facial expression, a momentary action, etc. Here is a typical example. The encapsulated narration is italicized:

> "The wind's rising," she said. "I fastened the window. Rosie is fast asleep." *Her gaze fell on the tray. It contained a mug of cocoa and a small plate of sandwiches.*
>
> *Guy followed her glance.* "By way of an apology for my bad temper," he said, "and because I suspect you didn't stop for much of a break on the way back from London. If you open your door I'll carry it in for you. Then I'll leave you in peace."

The encapsulated segment includes the turnover, 'Guy followed her glance'. This is one of those instances in which a little business with food and drink helps the narrative along. There is a kind of eye-contact for people who are embarrassed with each other, not-yet-lovers who have quarrelled. The speakers exchange looks by *looking at the food*: 'Her gaze fell on the tray . . . Guy followed her glance.' Note how the heroine's gaze acts for the heroine, and how the hero pursues her, though they are

both standing stock-still on the stairs. She avoids, he chases –
and all over a small plate of sandwiches.

(c) 'Hopalongs'. These are comment-sentences of the turnover type, breaking up what would otherwise be a passage of
monologue. Protracted monologue is not common in magazine
fiction; possibly editors underestimate their readers' tolerance to
extended blocks of text, or perhaps authors are unwilling to let
their characters talk for long without some intervening snippet
of description. Short monologues are often made to 'hop along'
from speech to speech, over hops from comment to comment:

> "It was the brake," she said. She felt weak and sick with
> shock. "Mrs Harris said the front brake was stiff but I forgot."
> Her teeth were beginning to chatter. "Oh, Guy, it's Rosie. I
> can't find her. I've searched and searched." A sudden hope
> came. "Have you been home? Has she been found?"

The hopalong comments – 'She felt weak and sick with shock',
'Her teeth were beginning to chatter', 'A sudden hope came' –
are regularly interpolated, and provide a narrative running parallel with the speeches. A variant of the device is the 'one-hop',
a single comment explaining a reaction or indicating a gesture,
punctuating a sequence of two or three utterances:

> "Of course not. I was forgetting." Sophy looked contrite.
> "Sisters are apt to be terrible matchmakers."
> "Are they?" Carmel forced a smile. "If your brother did
> marry, wouldn't you find it a bit lonely?" Carmel asked.
> "Lonely? My dear, I would relish the freedom!" Sophy half-
> closed her eyes as if bringing into focus a vista of imperishable
> delights. "Do you know my greatest ambition?"

Here two of the hop-comments – 'Sophy looked contrite',
'Carmel forced a smile' – might be transformed into adverbial
tags or participle clauses: 'Sophy said, looking contrite', 'Carmel
said, forcing a smile', 'Carmel said, with a forced smile'. The
third one-hop, 'Sophy half-closed her eyes as if . . .', is more
elaborate, yet shares, through its 'as if', the same character of
adverbiality.

(d) 'Inserts'. Narrative comments are inserted into the reporting phrases of dialogue, in the way illustrated above. The expan-
sion of the manner adverb into an adverbial clause is not
uncommon:

"When will you be back, Guy?" she asked, so quietly that
he had to bend to hear her.

But the most frequent insert formula is a sequence of reporting
verb plus manner adverb plus participle clause:

"Not too keen, eh?" the girl commented shrewdly, scrutinizing Sarah's face.

In many such instances the manner adverb might be omitted,
though adverb and present participle commonly occur in tandem
when the writer wishes to convey the *how* and the *what* of a
reaction, the mental state and the physical response. In an alternative formula, the reporting verb is tagged by a verbless adjectival clause – e.g. ' "I don't understand," she faltered, her face
ashen', – or a past participle used adjectivally – ' "It's ruined!"
she gasped, appalled'.

Participial inserts are regularly used to denote actions, or document states of mind, often in such a way as to constitute minimal
patches of narrative or characterization. For instance, this:

"But she loved Fergus," said Jane, determined not to be
drawn into his gloom.

Or this, in which the participle clause and its subordinates combine the functions of character-sketch and conversational turn-
out:

"Tell me about your new grandson, Mrs Harris," she said,
guessing correctly that the subject would engross Mrs Harris
for quite some time.

Or this:

"I quite forgot my key to the back door," she explained,
amazing herself at the glibness with which she told the untruth.

Such examples point to the role of the insert in the general
narrative pattern, as a moment of linkage between Dialogue and
Relation. There are other overlaps, already mentioned in passing, in the stylistic repertoire of these two narrative elements; in
dialogic structure, a turnover often has a narrative content similar
to that of a hopalong or an encapsulation in relational structure.
By such means, the modes of Dialogue and Relation are made
to intersect.

Syntactic clichés: 'adverbiality' and 'participiality'

A few grammatical forms and structures are put to such continual use in popfiction that they form a groundwork of narrative cliché. Adverbs, adverbial phrases, and adverbial clauses are virtually indispensable to the stylistic strategy; verbless adjectival clauses (as in 'Utterly speechless, she turned away') occur frequently; and participle clauses lie so thick on the page that their deletion would leave a bleak and disjointed narrative. The recurrent convergence of adverbial, adjectival, and participial constructions is illustrated by this brief patch:

> She recognized Simon Doe's back even before he turned to the bar, revealing his profile. She hesitated, unsure whether or not to speak to him. Then her mind was made up as a tall, fashionably dressed girl came to stand possessively beside him.

Remove the dependent constructions from this, and we are left with 'She recognized Simon Doe's back ... She hesitated ... then her mind was made up'. But it is in just those dependent constructions that the narrative is amplified and its actions effectively staged as events located in time and involving the attitudinal response of an observer. Adverbial or participial structures convey significant information to the reader thus:

Construction	Category	Significance
even before he turned to the bar	adverbial	temporal (signalled by 'before')
revealing his profile	participial	action by the observed
unsure whether or not to speak to him	adjectival	attitude of the observer
as a tall ... girl came to stand ... beside him	adverbial	temporal (signalled by 'as' + result ('to stand' etc.)

The adverbial clause concluding the paragraph incorporates an infinitive clause ('to stand' etc.), which in its turn incorporates a manner adverb ('possessively'). And the infinitive clause itself is adverbial, expressing a *purpose*. The author might have written 'a tall, fashionably dressed girl *came and stood* possessively beside him'; except, perhaps, that in doing so she would have ignored one of the perpetual concerns of magazine fiction, which is to show characters acting busily and significantly, even in mundane and fleeting circumstances. 'The girl came and stood' is less purposeful, and therefore marginally less eventful, than 'the girl came to stand'.

The show of activity is made so often through adverb or participle that one might speak of 'adverbiality' and 'participiality' as characteristic properties of style in the popular romance. Adverbial constructions steer readers through transitional patches of narrative; manner adverbs accompany them through the dialogue:

> Auntie Dier tapped her fingers with impatience as she listened to the ringing tone. Eventually, there was an answer.
> "Good morning, Kate!" said the older woman, cheerily.

This is surely not meant to be read with close attention; dwelling on it provokes mischievous enquiries – do you tap your fingers *patiently*?; when you have dialled your number, what else is there to *listen to* but the ringing tone?; and if you are a character in a short story, using the telephone to speak to another character, is it not reasonable to suppose that an answer will come *eventually*? Why all this descriptive fuss over a phone call? It could be done quite straightforwardly:

> Auntie Dier dialled Kate's number. "Good morning!" she said.

That, however, misses the major purpose of popstyling, which is to promote constantly the illusion of significant activity on the part of characters who twitch with life – impatient life, cheery life, a tapping, rapping, drumming life that makes an event out of lifting a receiver.

A fairly common device for brightening or heightening the narrative is to 'front', or 'pre-pose' adverbial constructions, especially adverbial phrases expressing manner or state of mind, e.g.:

> With a disarming grin he pressed a kiss on her lips.

(A nice example of the triumph of vivacity over verisimilitude; try kissing while grinning disarmingly.) Or again:

> With an odd sense of precognition, she knew it was Guy.

Not 'She guessed it was Guy' (he has almost run over her with his motor car), or even 'Somehow she knew it was Guy', but *With an odd sense of precognition* . . .; she is involved in a special kind of activity; she is 'precognizing', which is a strenuous species of 'recognizing', even while she lies with abraded knees beside her fallen bicycle. The adjectives in such constructions are often cliché-signals, anticipating the reader's responses. Why did she let herself be kissed (kissing is a serious matter in magazine fiction)?; because she was *disarmed* by his grin. ('Grin' is a word that carries an honest licence; a 'disarming smirk', or a 'disarming leer' would hardly be acceptable.) And is not this 'precognition' business a little strange, not to say exaggerated?; indeed, yes, but it is recognized as *odd*. In such ways the 'pre-posed' adverbial phrases both anticipate and key the reactions of the reader.

Participial constructions may also be pre-posed or post-posed. Post-positioning is the necessary rule in the reporting of dialogue, but in descriptions the choice is open, and it generally correlates with specific stylistic purposes. Compare the following:

(a) She lay half-stunned, her knees stinging.
(b) Stunned, Holly realised what she had thought about his behaviour.

In the first of these, the participle clause *amplifies*; in the second, it *emphasizes*. More precisely, the dependent clause in (a) extends the reference of the verb in the main clause ('lay . . . her knees stinging'); in (b) it focuses attention on the subject, 'Holly'. The order of clauses in (a) might be reversed ('Her knees stinging, she lay half-stunned'), or (b) could be rewritten in the form 'Holly realised, stunned, what she had thought about his behaviour'. In either case the 'meaning' of the sentence would be unchanged, but the relational perspective would be altered.

Here are some instances of post-posed participle clauses. In most of these examples the participial construction is equivalent to a co-ordinate clause introduced by 'and':

(a) She shifted in her seat, eying Sarah with interest.
    (= 'and eyed Sarah'; note *eying* – an important activity)
(b) She waited, holding her breath without realising that she did so.
    (= 'She waited and held her breath'; or 'While she waited she held her breath'; holding your breath is an activity of

sorts, but you are bound to realize fairly quickly that you
are doing it.)

(c) In silence she did so, flicking the switch and flooding the
room with light.
(= 'She put the light on'; 'flicking' and 'flooding' make a
drama out of a domestic commonplace.)

(d) Carmel rose to go, forcing a bright smile for the man who
watched her over his spectacle lenses.
    Outside, she sat in her car for a moment, resting her
head against the cold steering wheel.
(A typical patch of participiality. Note how the verb in the
participle clause 'amplifies' the main clause verb: 'rose . . .
forcing a bright smile', 'sat . . . resting her head'. Note
also the adjectival heightening of the drama; the smile is
'bright', the steering wheel is 'cold'.)

In another kind of participial narration, there is a switch of
subject in the dependent clause, with a narrowing of reference
from a person to some part of that person's body or clothing or
perceptual life:

(a) She was plunged into a nightmare, all her strength ebbing
until her whole body was trembling.
('Plunged' prompts the ocean-metaphor of 'ebbing'; 'all'
predicts 'whole'.)

(b) When Holly came to the steep hill that led to the moors,
she dismounted and trudged up it, her sandalled feet slopping through inches of water.
(There is sometimes a perceptible harmony of meaning
between verbs in the main and dependent clauses; thus
here, 'trudged [up]' 'harmonizes' with 'slopping [through]'.)

(c) She watched him striding away, his broad upper back
tapering to a lean waist and hips, his well-brushed glossy
dark hair just touching the back of his shirt collar.
(The participle clauses here embody recipe-descriptions
for the approved male of the magazine illustrations; he is
lean, well-kempt, and his hair is the currently fashionable
length. Once again, there is a 'harmonic' principle in the
sequence of verbs. He 'strides'; but his back is comparably
active, for it 'tapers'; and his hair reaches down and
'touches'. The man vibrates in all his parts.)

The pre-posed participle clause tends to focus attention dramatically on the subject of the main clause. This is particularly true of the past participle:

(a) Silhouetted in the lighted doorway, the man cast a giant shadow across the yard.

(The position of the participle clause is in this instance logically dictated. To write 'The man cast a giant shadow across the yard, silhouetted in the lighted doorway' would be to put the effective cart before the causal horse.)

(b) Alerted by sudden small gusts of wind, Deirdre Shackleton looked up.

(But here there is no logical compulsion to put the participle clause first.)

(c) Shaken by the directness of words which echoed her own recent thoughts, Sarah was embarrassed.

(Here the device is clumsily used; the subordinate clause is so much longer than its principal that the sentence becomes front-heavy, and any 'focusing' effect is lost. Furthermore, 'embarrassed' is no better than a feeble synonym of 'shaken'. The author might have described her heroine's plight more compactly: 'Sarah was shaken by the directness of words which echoed her own recent thoughts.' But the conventional semantics of this kind of narrative require two stages: an *event* – being 'shaken' – and a psychological *consequence* – feeling 'embarrassed'. The pattern is that of 'Hit by a brick, Jack was outraged', or 'Run over by the bus that was carrying her friends to the barbecue, Sally was mortified'.)

The pre-posed present participle is a general mannerism. A few examples:

(a) Smiling, Katy nodded.

(This could as well be 'Katy nodded, smiling', or 'Katy, smiling, nodded' – or even 'Nodding, Katy smiled', not to mention 'Katy smiled and nodded'. The point is to enregister what Katy *did*; and here she has two actions to her credit – a smile and a nod.)

(b) Scratching his head, the elderly locksmith stared at the back of the door.

(Or, 'Staring at the back of the door, the elderly locksmith scratched his head'; once again, it hardly matters – as long as 'scratching' and 'staring' are registered.)

(c) Rising abruptly, Carmel went to the front door where the locksmith was putting the finishing touches to his work.
(Here logic requires the pre-posing of the participle clause.)

(d) Feeling happier and more secure now the locks were to be changed, Carmel settled down to write a chatty letter to Samantha.
(Here it does not; but 'feeling happier' in the pre-position is a kind of focused attribute, not the mere additional comment it undoubtedly is in the post-position.)

(e) Squaring her shoulders, she pressed the bell with a resolute finger.
(= 'She rang the bell resolutely'. She could hardly press the bell with an *irresolute* finger; but 'resolute' follows in the lexical chain after 'squaring her shoulders'.)

(f) Arriving home, her happiness turned to anger in a flash.

(g) Inclining her head graciously as she introduced herself, it was obvious she felt she was doing Green Gables an honour by favouring it with her presence.
(The last two sentences exemplify the error of the misrelated participle, which occurs quite commonly. Probably the authors do not feel it to be an error, but perceive the participle clause in instances such as these as a kind of 'presentation', emphatically marking a point in time, a gesture, etc.)

(h) Glancing round her, Sarah's eyes took in the large clock on the façade of the building, and she noted that it had stopped.
(This is semi-syntactic – a blend of 'Glancing round, Sarah's eyes took in the large clock', etc., and 'Glancing round her, Sarah noted that the clock had stopped'. The blurring of the syntax follows from a confusion of semantic roles. Which is the operative *agent* – Sarah, or her eyes?)

The pre- and post-positioning of participle clauses is sometimes used to contour, or set out, short patches of description, as in the following instance:

Keeping their hats on and staying close to the beer, the men swapped stories, moaned about the drought and stole sly glances at Kate.

The women formed another group, complaining about their

husbands, discussing their children, catching up on the latest gossip.

The first sentence of this patch has pre-posed participle clauses; in the second, the dependent clauses are post-positioned. What this does is to trace a kind of syntactic boundary round the little tableau, in which the men and the women are adjacently grouped in the centre while the perimeter is occupied by a description of their behaviour. (Not uncharacteristically, it is the behavioural stereotype that claims the reader's attention; the men and women are all but anonymous.)

The narrative sentence: sequences and syntheses

The frequency of adverbial and participial constructions greatly affects the telling of the magazine story, in its progression from sentence to sentence. Rarely does the narrative proceed in a series of simple steps, like this:

> A low rumble of thunder pealed around the house. It went on for a long time. The sky had darkened dramatically.

A short sequence of simple sentences is a mark of dramatic heightening, presenting information step by step. It is much more common for information to be rolled up into the dependent clauses of a complex sentence:

> As Holly went up the stairs to check on her sister, who was staying at Gregory's while their parents had taken the weekend off to visit a festival of flowers, she couldn't still her tumbling thoughts.

This, the first sentence of a serial instalment, 'synthesizes' the immediate narration ('Holly had tumbling thoughts while walking upstairs') with information of which the reader may need to be reminded. A lot of sentences or descriptive patches are synthetic in this way, and the syntheses occur quite often when the writer is trying to negotiate a 'natural' transition in the narrative:

> Eventually, Jane drained the last dregs from her coffee cup and was astonished to see, when she glanced at her wrist-watch, that it was almost ten o'clock. Letting herself out of the dining room into the echoing hall, she remembered that

she had finished her novel earlier in the day, and decided to
take up Alexander's invitation to use the library.

Jane finishes her coffee; Jane notices that it is almost ten o'clock;
Jane goes to the library to get another novel. But that is not it
at all! Jane is *busy*! She *drains* the last dregs from her coffee
cup, she *glances* at her wristwatch, she *lets herself out* of the
dining room, she *decides* to take up an invitation to use the
library. At this effortful rate she will be overcome before she sets
foot on the stair. (But she is in for a shock: 'In a brightly-lit alcove,
surrounded by the trappings of a modern office, Alexander was
slumped over his desk, unconscious.' He has dozed off over the
accounts.) There are three reasons for this synthetic busyness:
first, she is a heroine, and no heroine worth her salt would ever
simply drink her coffee and leave the room; second, the reader
must be reminded that this is a *big* house, with *big* rooms, and
doors you have to *push*; and thirdly, the author is a little foxed
by the problem of getting Jane out of the dining room, where
she has been enjoying an informative chat with Mrs Brixham,
the housekeeper, and up to the library, where her romantic
employer is slumped among the office trappings, waiting for a
phone call from Central America. (He has to explain to Jane
what time zones are, although she is bright and speaks 'several
languages, as well as French'.) These factors collectively require
the synthetic syntax, an artifice for keeping the reader in touch
with the domestic facts of romantic life, and for hustling the
heroine through meals, out of rooms, and up staircases. Every
movement, it seems, must be accounted for, every piece of
commonplace action quite emphatically noted. It would never
do to write 'Jane finished her dinner and went upstairs to get a
book'. To the reader, apparently, is attributed the scrupulous
inquisitiveness of the child who has to know what happens *at
every step*, and who cannot regard the tale as properly told if
the slightest detail is omitted. If that is so, however, it poses a
problem for the writers of magazine fiction. They are required
to satisfy the curiosity of the child – or the simple gossip – but
in a style thought appropriate to the sophistication of the adult.
The participle clauses that occur so frequently in magazine fiction
are one symptom of a striving for the sophisticated style.

The lexicon

A recurrent striving after effect is also apparent in the lexicon of
these magazine stories; the effect of vivacity, of decisive emphasis, of an activity or a perceptual sharpness often in excess of
what the simple facts of the narrative would presuppose. Thus
when the heroine of the story quoted above finds her employer
in the library, face down among the balance sheets, we are told:

> Jane ran across the room to him, but as soon as her hand
> touched his cheek, his eyes opened.

All that the sentence has to do is note the movement from the
door to the desk. Something of this sort might have served well
enough:

> Jane went to him, but as soon as she touched his cheek, he
> opened his eyes.

The original, however, differs from this in two ways, both of
which have to do with the paradoxical busyness and helplessness
of the magazine heroine. On the one hand, the vocabulary is
'upgraded', so that Jane neither *goes* nor *walks*, but *runs*. (Not
because the author wants to remind us of the size of the house
and its rooms, but because she wants to project the emotional
vitality of her heroine.) On the other hand, Jane is seemingly
robbed of volition; it is not *she*, but *her hand* that touches the
sleeper's cheek. This fairly unremarkable sentence involves, in
fact, two of the commonest lexical-semantic devices in magazine
fiction: *upgrading* and *agent-shift*.

   Upgrading is of two kinds. One consists of rejecting the central
vocabulary item, or notional head of a synonym set (e.g. 'go')
in favour of a stronger or more specific member of the set (e.g.
'run', 'rush', 'dash', 'fly', 'scuttle'). This type of upgrading is
seen most frequently in verbs of motion, verbs of cognition and
perception, verbs denoting a response. The heroine may 'look',
but she is just as likely to 'stare', 'glare', 'gaze', 'scrutinize',
'glower', or 'shoot a glance'. Her tears may 'flow', but generally
'spring' to her eyes before 'streaming', or 'coursing', or even
'pouring' down her cheeks. Descriptive patches of otherwise
quite banal import take a spurious impression of significance
from the upgraded verb:

> In the foyer of the hotel, Andrew Campbell rose from the

bench seat and Claire, shocked, stumbled forward, staring at
him, disbelieving.

Claire does not 'walk', nor does she 'step'; she 'stumbles'
(coming fresh from the experience of being embraced by a man
of dubious character). She does not 'look', she 'stares'; and –
with a commensurate upgrading of participles – she is not
'startled' and 'surprised', but 'shocked' and 'disbelieving'.

The second type of upgrading is distinguished by the inclusion
of metaphor in the attempt at forceful expression:

> Kate was rooted to the spot, caught up in whirling emotions.
> As she tried to understand the strength of the feelings that
> Nick had triggered off, guilt clawed at her.

What is upgraded here might be paraphrased thus:

> Kate, full of emotion, stood quite still. As she tried to under-
> stand the strong feelings that Nick had aroused in her, she felt
> guilty.

But the paraphrase omits any intimation of those overwhelming
forces that incapacitate the heroine: the whirlwind, the detonation, the wild beast. She is to be represented both as the centre
of vigorous action and at the same time as a hapless victim; her
role often shifts from the *agentive* to the *patientive*.

Upgrading and agent-shift are thus interrelated devices. The
latter occurs when the apparent agent in the clause – commonly
the referent of the grammatical subject – is either non-animate
or is part of the human body. Examples are frequent, and sometimes unintentionally comic:

> A torpedo of anxiety shot through her system.
> Hot anger trembled through her body.
> Panic throttled her.
> She sighed, a great peace creeping over her.
> She sat on the edge of a hotel bed, tears tightening her throat.
> Claire turned abruptly, going back into the house, remorse
> burning her as hotly as the sun had done.
> His hand was on her bare shoulder, and it slid beneath the
> shoulder strap, savouring her bare skin as though his fingers
> had tongues. A clamour of desire rose in her, destroying her
> cool control.

In each of these instances, the agent-shift is accompanied by an
additional turn of metaphor, sometimes startlingly original, as in

the first example, sometimes quite commonplace. (The tears that 'tighten the throat', for example, occur repeatedly in magazine fiction.) Such metaphors usually hinge on the verb, and the metaphoric loading of the verb is another kind of upgrading.

In general, the purpose of figurative language in these stories for women is to raise stylistic energy. Rarely do we find any subtle exploitation of symbolism, any exploration of the possibilities of metaphor or patterns of imagery that inform the whole narrative. Instead, there is a persistent use of metaphoric cliché, a parading of a few figurative devices with the aim of infusing energy, excitement, interest, into almost every line of the narrative. Packing the verb with metaphoric vitality (as when a hand 'savours' bare skin) is one favourite tactic; another is the fairly frequent use of similes; a third is the recurrent use of descriptions introduced by the phrases 'as if' and 'as though'. These expressions, which are ordinarily used to introduce an elucidation or a reformulation (for instance, 'He felt tongue-tied, as though he had forgotten every word of English he ever knew'), are also the operators that pile the improbable on the unlikely. Emphasis, rather than explanation, is the frequent purpose of 'as if' in magazine fiction. The following is perhaps an extreme example:

> But it was as if the last few days had soaked her will in a lassitude that weighed down her ability to make any decision at all.

This hardly explains her inability to make decisions, nor does it provide an analogy that might convincingly help the reader to understand her mental state. It tells us that her will was not simply weak, or inert, or sluggish, but 'soaked' in lassitude; in fact the 'as if' is merely the preliminary marker to a piece of upgrading.

Again and again – many examples have been given already – the compulsion to upgrade leads to writing in excess of what is needed; and this in its turn leads to frequent cliché. For example:

> His blue eyes seemed to pierce through her and she battled to hold on to her equanimity.

'Battling to hold on to one's equanimity' upgrades 'fighting for self-control', which in its turn upgrades 'trying to keep calm'. But battles imply war, and war implies weapons, and weapons

can 'pierce' – like the blue gaze of innumerable magazine men.
Another instance:

> Elderthorpe was basking in late afternoon sunshine when Jane
> wandered out of the drawing room onto the terrace. She drew
> a deep breath of the balmy air and gazed out appreciatively
> at the peaceful garden.

This is the opening of a serial episode of *The Governess* –
the story of Jane, whose lightest movement is stamped with
significance. Its function is simply to establish a place, a time,
and a person – a common operation at the beginning of a
narrative – but it has pretensions which evidently go beyond the
simple statement 'One sunny afternoon, Jane went out onto the
terrace at Elderthorpe'. The ordinary act is upgraded – she
wanders, she breathes, she gazes appreciatively – and the setting
itself is descriptively heightened – the house basks, the air is
balmy, the garden is peaceful. The result is not a heightening of
perceptive power, but merely the inflation of cliché.

The cliché, however, is arguably one of the strengths of magazine narration, a predictable feature of style accommodated to
predictable features of structure, making for rapid and secure
reading. At the moment of False Perception, we may expect that
the heroine will experience 'a turmoil of emotions', or that she
will 'blink back tears'; just as, in consequence of the Clarifying
Act, it may be noted that happiness 'bubbles up inside her'.
Often these phrases are not so much descriptions as little signa-
tures attesting to the progress of the story. Occasionally they may
be elaborated by some figurative extension naïvely suggested by
the cliché-word:

> Laughter was bubbling up inside her, a happiness as fizzy as
> champagne.

'Bubble' touches off 'bubbly' – whence 'champagne' – which is
'fizzy'; associative processes of this kind occur quite often (and
in some cases unintentionally) in magazine style.

The figurative vocabulary of the stories thus depends on a
primary vocabulary which itself consists of spent metaphors or
conventional descriptive tokens. Adjectives, obviously, are an
important form-class, of which three semantic types occur
frequently:

(a) Adjectives of sensory perception: colour words, participial adjectives expressing intensities of light ('glittering', 'gleaming', 'sparkling'), or of sound ('tinkling', 'roaring'), words descriptive of texture ('rough', 'smooth', 'soft', 'silky'), words denoting tactile impressions ('hard', 'soft', 'warm', 'cool', 'sharp'), words denoting dimension or bodily shape ('long', 'round', 'broad', 'slim', 'lean'). Such words are extensively used, in descriptions of dress and physical appearance, or in the occasional demure venture into the erotic.

(b) Terms denoting the responses and emotional states of the fictional characters – e.g. 'furious', 'anxious', 'affectionate', 'despairing', 'cold', 'resolute', 'wavering'. Many of these have corresponding manner adverbs, and either the adjective or the adverb or both may occur in collocation with an upgraded verb: 'she shot a furious glance at Tom', 'his cold blue eyes transfixed her with an icy stare', 'she shrank miserably into herself', 'her loving eyes laughed up at him trustingly'.

(c) Terms suggesting an appropriate response from the *reader*, e.g. 'heart-warming', 'thrilling', 'appalling'. These adjectives are ambivalent in function; they suggest that the heroine is 'thrilled' (for example), while telling the reader to feel 'thrilled' on the heroine's behalf. This can also apply to words denoting physical features of shape and colour, which in the appropriate context can be used to enlist the reader's emotional support. In romantic fiction, words like 'small' and 'pale' – as in her small hands or her pale young face – are often made to exert a conspiratorial appeal.

Beyond the cliché

It is indeed the reader's conspiring assent to conventions of language and structure, to the quick-serve devices of cafeteria narrative, that establishes the magazine story, not as an art form so much as an industrial product. Cliché, elsewhere attributable to fatigue or lapse of creative attention, here becomes almost a dynamic principle; the stories, it seems, can only be written by someone with a deft command of cliché and the ability to take it quite seriously. And yet there are magazine stories – perhaps a growing number – that dispense with clichés of language, situation, and feeling. In these stories we often find writing that eludes the obvious label 'romantic fiction' and invites comparison with literary narrative of a rather less commercial kind. Here is an instance:

They never cried on that journey; they laughed and thought what great times they would have and they found a room near Paddington station and though they pretended to be married, they slept in separate rooms until they were married by an Italian priest, three weeks later, with two Italians as their witnesses.

She wrote one letter home. Early in that year, in the spring of 1963. She said that they had been married in a Catholic Church and that they had used the £1,200 to buy a share in a small corner shop. They thought the business should be very good.

They were both prepared to work long hours, and this was how you built up a good trade in a neighbourhood like this. She said she had nothing more to say, and she didn't really expect to hear from them, she thought they had said all they ever wanted to say that last day. But still Louis had been very keen that she should let them know where she was. Louis sent them cordial wishes. She was merely pleasing him by writing this once.

They wrote, they tried to write letters explaining what had been done was done with the best of motives. Nessa wrote and told her about the visit of President Kennedy and how they had all gone on the excursion to see him. Seamus wrote and said it was a bit dead at home now, and you'd sort of feel sorry for the old fella. But Mary never wrote back.

This passage from a story called 'Change of Heart', by Maeve Binchy (printed in *Woman*, December 17, 1983) declines the usual resources of magazine language. The manner adverb, the participial clause, the upgraded verb, the stereotyped adjective, the hack metaphor, have no part to play here. Certainly the piece could be analysed as a specimen of stylistic convention, but the conventions it uses are not those generally associated with the magazine story, and they do not sit well with the common structural pattern of changing perceptions, explanatory revelations, and final homecoming. The Christmas tale that Maeve Binchy has to tell is, in fact, not cast in the romantic mould, though it tells in its own way a story of coming Home.

In the same magazine issue there is one other story, by Sue Gee, called 'Someone Remembered'. This is also a story of homecoming and reunion, and it is stylistically unusual in that its narrative base is in the present tense; otherwise, however, it observes the conventions and protocols of magazine style. An extract:

> Jonathan is ill. He is also deeply unhappy. He has been ditched. Three weeks ago he rang his loving family to tell them he would be bringing someone down for Christmas. There was a slight pause as his sister took in this announcement.
>
> "Oh," she said. "Hang on a tick. I'll get Ma."
>
> Their mother came to the phone. "Darling? Sandy says you're bringing someone down . . . lovely, of course . . . who is it, exactly?"
>
> "It's a wonderful girl called Susanna." Jonathan put out a hand to stroke the casually cut tresses of the object of his desire as she went past. She gave him a lazy smile and drifted into the bedroom. "You'll love her, Mother," he said firmly.
>
> Again, as with his sister, there was a slight but discernible something passing down the wires.
>
> "Mother?"
>
> "Yes, dear. Yes, of course, I'm sure I shall. It's just that . . . we . . . what about Georgina?"
>
> "What?"
>
> "Well, you know she's coming over . . . and we're going over there . . . and . . . er . . ."
>
> "Mother," said Jonathan, "I thought we'd done that one. I'll ring you later."
>
> Later, when Susanna had gone to meet a friend for a drink, departing in a cloud of exotic and infinitely desirable scent, and wearing the exquisitely cut trousers Jonathan had bought for her the previous weekend, he rang his home again.

This passage is taken from the one section of the narrative written in the past tense – a 'dilative' episode without the usual linguistic symptoms of Dilation (though the tell-tale past perfective occurs here and there). The dialogue is presented without an obvious framework of 'turn' devices, and there is some attempt at naturalistic reporting of the hesitations and false starts of everyday speech. Yet cliché lurks everywhere: in the 'casually cut tresses' and the 'exquisitely cut trousers'; in 'the object of his desire' and the 'lazy smile' – for who smiles industriously?; in 'he said firmly'; in the upgrading of 'drifted'; in the busy participiality of 'departing in a cloud of exotic and infinitely desirable scent, and wearing the exquisitely cut trousers Jonathan had bought for her the previous weekend'. The extract from Maeve Binchy's story lies beyond cliché; this last passage lies just a little beyond, but not very far.

In most examples of magazine fiction, the stylistic limit is quickly reached and understood. The genre on the whole concedes little to adventurousness in ideas or language. It tends to prescribe roles of femininity, and thus to imply corresponding roles of masculinity. Above all, its plots draw circumscribing lines round woman's potential for action and independence. Its heroines are not so much passive, or inactive, as deprived of initiative. They are compelled to respond to circumstances imposed upon them; they are powerless and defensive. This defensiveness is generally reflected in the style of the stories told about them. And what remarkable lies these stories do succeed in telling – what a world of dolls and cardboard it is that can so represent yet so resist all reality! For here you are, my dear, with your hair softly cascading over your nose, and here am I transfixing you with my mockingly bloodshot gaze, and there is Professor Pangloss with his kindly old eyes screwed shut, and his grizzled old head lolling down, and his wise old mouth full ajar, and his seat comfortably tilted right back into the knees of the fat lady behind him. We are all candidates for someone's fiction, no doubt, but I do not think our stains and distasteful frailties will let us through the coloured door that admits the beautiful people to Elderthorpe or Gregory's or Cranmere Park. Nor shall we live with Holly and Summer and tall, dark, hazel-eyed, sarcastic Dr Simon Harraday. No, indeed. But look, here is our stewardess in her smart cross-over apron, cheerfully pushing a big metal trolley. They are handing out lunch; and not before time, say I.

3 Man's business: a look round the action story

> but man, proud man,
> Dress'd in a little brief authority, –
> Most ignorant of what he's most assured,
> His glassy essence – like an angry ape,
> Plays such fantastic tricks before high heaven
> As make the angels weep.
> (Shakespeare, *Measure for Measure*)

So, madam, now that I have criticized your reading matter and we have jostled and squirmed our way through the plastic luncheon, I think it prudent, before the film begins, to join the line here, if you will pardon me. They are mostly men, as you see, some with their shaving bags already, and some wearing caps and carpet slippers – will you look at them? – this one with his cigarette furtively cupped in his fist, and that one with his undefended cough, and the other with the turned-down waistband and a paunch that peeps whitely through an unbuttoned gap in his tartan shirt. This is my sex, heaven help me. Good men, maybe, adequate husbands, benevolent fathers, conscientious bread-winners, honest, charitable, right-thinking men – but shall we ever be heroes? Shall we defend the beleaguered outpost, swim underwater to plant the limpet mine, outface the cattle baron's hired gun, beat the syndicate to the manganese deposits, go into enemy territory knowing that Mother will Deny All Knowledge Of Us if we are caught? Not if this toilet queue is anything to go by. We have the likes of Fleming and Forsyth and Maclean and Innes and Robert Ludlum and Wilbur Smith and the rest of them to do and dare on our behalf.

The actionbook (a good enough name for the genre) helps the ordinary man in the aisle to fill in one or two gaps. It makes him technologically competent, and grants him the ingenuity to solve desperately complicated problems, alone, or with minor assistance from his associates, or perhaps even in their despite.

It enables him to enjoy fast cars, fast women, prodigious meals, fabulous resorts, and furious fights, without suffering a coronary attack or falling out with his wife and having to sleep in the box-room. It allows him limitless snobbery, arrogance, chauvinism, and homicidal excess. It makes him a survivor, and more than a survivor, a winner. If there are rewards and honours, he gets them. If there are none, he at least has the comfort of knowing that he has witnessed the triumph of righteousness. Through magfiction, women are offered the joy of Coming Home; in the actionbook, men experience the stern satisfaction of Winning Through. Comrades perish, the homestead is burned, the woman is intractably proud, the villain slips away into the darkness crying 'I shall be back', but the hero, Jack-in-the-middle, comes through it all with a peculiar conviction of one thing: that glassy essence, his identity.

In popular fiction, the identity of the hero (and often of other prominent characters) is signalled insistently to the reader, who is not permitted to neglect the distinction between attendant persons and central personages. The following passage from James Clavell's *King Rat* illustrates one of the ways in which this may be done. The scene is a Japanese prisoner of war camp. An American soldier, known throughout the book as the King, because his peculiar entrepreneurial talents have enabled him to establish a profitable ascendancy over his environment and his fellow-prisoners, notices a young man deep in conversation with a Malay. Impressed by the young man's evident linguistic ability, the King sends a henchman to fetch him:

Max slipped out of the window and crossed the path. "Hey, Mac," he said abruptly to the young man. "The King wants to see you," and jerked a thumb towards the hut. "On the double."

The man gaped at Max, then followed the line of the thumb to the American hut. "Me?" he asked incredulously, looking back at Max.

"Yeah, you." Max said impatiently.

"What for?"

"How the hell do I know?"

The man frowned at Max, hardening. He thought a moment, then turned to Suliman, the Malay. "Nantih-lah," he said.

"Bik, tuan," said Suliman, preparing to wait. Then he added in Malay, "Watch thyself, tuan. And go with God."

"Fear not, my friend – but I thank thee for thy thought," the man said, smiling. He got up and followed Max into the hut.

"You wanted me?" he asked, walking up to the King.

"Hi," the King said, smiling. He saw that the man's eyes were guarded. That pleased him, for guarded eyes were rare. "Take a seat." He nodded at Max, who left. Without being asked, the other men who were near moved out of earshot so the King could talk in private.

"Go on, take a seat," the King said genially.

"Thanks."

"Like a cigarette?"

The man's eyes widened as he saw the Kooa offered to him. He hesitated, then took it. His astonishment grew as the King snapped the Ronson, but he tried to hide it and drew deeply on the cigarette. "That's good. Very good," he said luxuriously. "Thanks".

"What's your name?"

"Marlowe. Peter Marlowe." Then he added ironically, "And yours?"

The King laughed. Good, he thought, the guy's got a sense of humour, and he's no ass kisser. He docketed the information, then said, "You're English?"

"Yes."

The King had never noticed Peter Marlowe before, but that was not unusual when ten thousand faces looked so much alike. He studied Peter Marlowe silently and the cool blue eyes studied him back.

"Kooas are about the best cigarette around," the King said at last. "'Course they don't compare with Camels. American cigarette. Best in the world. You ever had them?"

"Yes," Peter Marlowe said, "but actually, they tasted a little dry to me. My brand's Gold Flake." Then he added politely, "It's a matter of taste, I suppose." Again a silence fell and he waited for the King to come to the point. As he waited, he thought that he liked the King, in spite of his reputation, and he liked him for the humour that glinted behind his eyes.

"You speak Malay very well," the King said, nodding at the Malay who waited patiently.

"Oh, not too badly, I suppose."

The King stifled a curse at the inevitable English underplay. "You learn it here?" he asked patiently.

"No. In Java. Peter Marlowe hesitated and looked around. "You've quite a place here."

"Like to be comfortable. How's that chair feel?"

"Fine." A flicker of surprise showed.

"Cost me eighty bucks," the King said. "Year ago."

Peter Marlowe glanced at the King sharply to see if it was meant as a joke, to tell him the price, just like that, but he saw only happiness and evident pride. Extraordinary, he thought, to say such a thing to a stranger. "It's very comfortable," he said, covering his embarrassment.

"I'm going to fix chow. You like to join me?"

"I've just had – lunch," Peter Marlowe said, carefully.

"You could probably use some more. Like an egg?"

Now Peter Marlowe could no longer conceal his amazement, and his eyes widened. The King smiled and felt that it had been worthwhile to invite him to eat to get a reaction like that. He knelt down beside his black box and carefully unlocked it.

Peter Marlowe stared down at the contents, stunned.

It has been necessary to quote at some length in order to demonstrate how Clavell establishes a simple stylistic device that governs the narrative throughout the book. This passage introduces the person who is to function as 'viewpoint character', or as one who principally mirrors the psychological power of the personality here called 'the King'. The character appears initially as 'a young man', then (at the beginning of the passage quoted above) as 'the young man', then as 'the man', and finally as 'Marlowe. Peter Marlowe'. Such a progression, from indefinite article to definite article to personal name is frequently observable in fiction of all kinds, as a way of bringing characters into the focus of the reader's attentions. What is striking in this case, however, is the continued repetition of the name Peter Marlowe – not familiarly 'Peter', or more formally 'Marlowe', but *Peter Marlowe*, again and again. Once the name has been introduced, it occurs no less than nine times in the quoted extract, and in the almost three hundred pages of the book that remain after this episode it will go on occurring in comparable density whenever this character enters the narrative – and he is very rarely out of it. We may notice, in the present instance, how the name finds its first syntactic role in the direct object slot, reflecting the fact that 'the young man' at first owes his identity to the interest

of 'the King' ('The King had never noticed Peter Marlowe before
. . .', 'He studied Peter Marlowe silently'). Fairly quickly, however, as 'the young man' becomes the observer of 'the King'
and his kingdom, the name begins to appear in the subject
position in declarative sentences, as well as in speech-reporting
clauses. ('Peter Marlowe hesitated and looked around', 'Peter
Marlowe glanced at the King sharply . . .', 'Now Peter Marlowe
could no longer contain his amazement . . .', 'Peter Marlowe
stared down at the contents, stunned'). The norm of reference
to these two characters is to 'Peter Marlowe' and 'the King'. The
latter (whom Marlowe sometimes addresses jokily as 'Rajah') is
called 'the King' throughout the book, and only in the closing
pages, after the camp is liberated, do we become aware that
King is his surname. (He is Corporal King.) His reversion to
ordinariness, the loss of the identity that the prison camp has
conferred upon him, is for him psychologically disabling:

> But the King only wanted to hide. Forsyth and the others had
> taken away his face. He knew that he was lost. And faceless,
> he was terrified.
> "See you around," he muttered and saluted and hurried
> away. Jesus God, he wept inside, give me back my face.
> Please give me back my face.

Appropriately, given the novel's context of action, the perceived
loss of commanding identity is expressed in Oriental terms, as
'loss of face'. The King rides out of the story ("Corporal!" an
angry sergeant tells him, "Get your goddam ass in the truck")
as an ordinary man among ordinary unidentified men:

> Meekly he got into the back of the truck and stood while
> everyone else sat, and around him there were excited men
> talking to one another, but not to him. No one seemed to
> notice him. He held to the side of the truck as it roared into
> life and swept the Changi dust into the air.

But Marlowe, though despairing and forsaken at the end, is
never 'faceless', and his identity is asserted to the very last in
the insistent repetition of his name:

> The first truck moved and the second and the third, and all
> the trucks left Changi, and only once did Peter Marlowe look
> back.
> When he was far away.

In this story by James Clavell (incidentally a very good story), the syntactically highlighted use of personal names is one of the stylistic keys to the book, which is concerned with the struggle to survive; Peter Marlowe and the King are survivors, who by their will to live stand out from the crowd. Other writers play the naming game less systematically, or do not include it in their stylistic repertoire. Names are important in Frederick Forsyth's thrillers, as agents of verisimilitude (the characters bear their names around as though they were forever presenting the reader with their passports) and sometimes as tokens distinguishing the leading figures from the lesser fry. A passage of dialogue from *The Devil's Alternative* illustrates a typical use of personal names in occasional variation with periphrastic reference (the identification of characters by means of phrases indicating nationality, occupation, physical peculiarity, etc.):

In a small flat in Bayswater, London, three men sat that day and stared at the tangle of newspapers strewn on the floor around them.

"A disaster," snapped Andrew Drake, "A bloody disaster. By now they should have been in Israel. Within a month they'd have been released and could have given their press conference. What the hell did they want to shoot the captain for?"

"If he was landing at Schönefeld and refused to fly into West Berlin, they were finished anyway," observed Azamat Krim.

"They could have clubbed him," snorted Drake.

"Heat of the moment," said Kaminsky. "What do we do now?"

"Can those handguns be traced?" asked Drake of Krim.

The small Tatar shook his head. "To the shop that sold them, perhaps," he said. "Not to me. I didn't have to identify myself."

Drake paced the carpet, deep in thought.

"I don't think they'll be extradited back," he said at length. "The Soviets want them now for hijacking, shooting Rudenko, hitting the KGB man on board and of course the other one they took the identity card from. Still, I don't think a West German government will send two Jews back for execution. On the other hand, they'll be tried and convicted. Probably to life. Miroslav, will they open their mouths about Ivanenko?"

The Ukrainian refugee shook his head.

Andrew Drake and Azamat Krim are identified in full, as befits leading members of the conspiratorial group whose activities provide the plot of the book. They are periodically referred to in this style, but not regularly. Here, for instance, the first statement of the full name is followed by references to the surname only. Kaminsky, slightly less important than the other two, is first mentioned by his surname and then by his forename (Miroslav); and both he and Krim, when required to shake their heads for the sake of dialogic realism, do so periphrastically ('The small Tatar shook his head', 'The Ukrainian refugee shook his head'). Characters in actionbooks, like the women in magfiction, have to put in a certain amount of nodding, frowning, smiling, or gesticulating at turnover junctures in dialogue.

The episode from which this extract is taken reveals quite incidentally a great deal about the author's penchant for names, and the importance of names in his style. Counting repetitions (which indeed are ingredients in the stiff onomastic pudding-mix of Mr Forsyth's style), there are 38 names in less than two pages of text: 17 personal names, 12 place names, 8 references to nationality, and 1 occupational title (the KGB man). Such density of designation is by no means untypical of this author in this book, every page of which is a clutter of names. In places the passion for noting what people, things, or places are called, verges on the comic:

> To those in the Anglo-American alliance of intelligence services, a strange and guarded, but ultimately vital, alliance, the SIS was always called "the firm". To its employees those in the counter-intelligence arm, the MI5, were "the colleagues". The CIA at Langley, Virginia, was "the company" and its staff "the cousins". On the opposite side worked "the opposition" whose headquarters was at Number 2, Dzerzhinsky Square, Moscow, named after the founder of the old Cheka, Feliks Dzerzhinsky, Lenin's secret police boss. This building would always be known as "the centre" and the territory east of the Iron Curtain as "the bloc".

Such writing has an effect on the reader analogous to the social habit of name-dropping: it either impresses or bores. Forsyth's unrelenting construction of reality by the naming of names may read at times like a tedious display of the author's painstaking researches into 'background' and 'period'. Every personage, every office, every institution is elaborately dossiered and labelled. Realism is the obvious goal, but not the sole consequence of all this naming. It has other functions, one of which is to compensate for the absence of anything like a subtle, perceptive examination of characters and relationships. Psychologically, the people in Forsyth's books dress in clichés and travel in stereotypes, but their banality is dazzlingly screened by names, names, names. Identity, fixed and repeatedly formulated, triumphs over the shifting truths and fugitive potential of character. There is, however, a poetic power of sorts lurking in the ramifications and reiterations of naming; gradually the reader is persuaded to feel the feelings the names purportedly connote, so that a passage like the one quoted above, discussing the familiar names of the great powers' intelligence services, becomes more than a piece of background realism, persuading us of the credentials of the story and its actors; it becomes in itself a stylistic and aesthetic experience, a not unshapely piece of prose creating a discernible pattern of rhetorical parallels and oppositions, a pattern in which the names are regularly, even symmetrically, located. (See, for instance, the placing of the alliterating items 'the company' and 'the cousins' in 'The CIA at Langley, Virginia, was "the company" and its staff "the cousins".') If, after all, this rhetoric prompts a smile, it is because sophisticated or 'literary' readers, whose approval may rightly be a matter of indifference to Mr Forsyth, perceive a discrepancy between style and content. A rendering of parts of the telephone directory into Ciceronian periods would make us laugh; what Forsyth does is not as silly as that, and is certainly not done with comic intention, but the effect is, none the less, mildly parodic.

The technological buzz; or figmental factuality

In actionbooks names lie next door to facts, and facts, particularly of a technological kind, are in their turn important as vouchers of trustworthy realism and as sources of fantasy. Some writers are unremittingly, almost comically precise, after the manner of journalistic reportage, about times, places, ages, distances, weights, measures. To quote Mr Forsyth again, the second chapter of his *The Devil's Alternative* begins as follows:

While Adam Munro was changing trains at Revolution Square

shortly before 11.a.m. that morning of 10th June, a convoy of a dozen sleek, black, Zil limousines was sweeping through the Borovitsky Gate in the Kremlin wall a hundred feet above his head and one thousand three hundred feet southwest of him. The Soviet Politburo was about to begin a meeting that would change history.

This introduction continues for almost two pages with a factual description of the architectural structure and political organiz- ation of the Kremlin. One paragraph, however, is enough to illustrate the device of using facts to force-feed the imagination. If we remove from this passage the names denoting persons, places, products, and institutions ('Adam Munro', 'Revolution Square', 'Borovitsky Gate', 'Kremlin', 'Zil', 'Soviet Politburo'), not too much remains. The content is even more grossly impaired if we then take away the expressions of time, number, and distance ('shortly before 11.a.m.', 'that morning of 10th June', 'a dozen', 'a hundred feet above his head', 'one thousand three hundred feet southwest of him'). Then we are left with the unremarkable message that some sleek, black limousines were bringing some people to a meeting. 'Sleek' and 'black' may not seem worth the adjectival effort (what are limousines when they are other than sleek? Rough? Coarse? Crude?), but the stylistic commitment of the passage is obviously not to these minor and wholly conventional descriptive touches. It is to the figment of factuality, to the excitement raised by reference to every boy's own book of little-known facts. Did you know that if you were to stand on the platform of the underground station at Revolution Square, Moscow, the wall of the Kremlin would be exactly one hundred feet above your head and one thousand three hundred feet to the south west of you? Anyone who can tell you that must know what he is talking about; we feel that we are there, in the very thick of things.

Facts and figures create the technological buzz that readers, or at any rate male readers, seem to find reassuring; while the engines are thus roaring the fictional machine must be safely aloft. Actionbook writers are consequently obliged to do a great deal of research and to reproduce particular and up-to-date information on a variety of matters: on the types and series- numbers of aircraft and motor vehicles, on the varieties and calibres of weapons and ammunition, on the tonnage and cargo capacity of ships, on the results of geological and hydrographic surveys, on the temperatures generated by thermic lances, on the construction of time-locks, on hydraulic rams, on the mechanics of lifts and elevators. This is erudition of a particular kind. Authors are rarely expected to know the Köchel numbers of Mozart piano sonatas, the location of major paintings by Tiepolo, or the contents of British Museum manuscript Cotton Vitellius A XV, because these eruditions are, on the whole, wimpish, while information of the other kind is, by and large, macho. The man in the aisle may never have discharged a Finnish-made Sako Hornet .22 (it fires soft-nosed 45 grain, hollow-point Remington shells, capable of high velocity and great penetration), nor will he have had much practice with a thermic lance, but he likes to be entrusted with the flattering possibility of understanding these things. In a man's world, men – even the man who is palpably at odds with his battery-powered razor – are on friendly terms with machines, walk at ease with Technology, and have at least shaken hands with Science.

As with the naming of names, the purpose of this technological display can go beyond mere realism and take on a communicative power at something like a symbolic level. Here is a remarkable extract from a book called *34 East*, by Alfred Coppel. Air Force One, the plane used by the President of the United States, is on a flight to Palm Springs, with the President aboard. The pilot, Colonel Dayton, has been feeling ill for some time. As the plane begins the run in to the airport, his symptoms of distress grow more acute. He is experiencing a heart attack:

Dayton was in severe pain now. The intima of the aortic arch was tearing, cell by cell, along the line of division, collapsing as the rift on the artery opened as though along a microscopic faultline. An unbearable pressure seemed to be building up under his breastbone, and he unlatched the shoulder harness with clawing hands. He could hear Campbell shouting something in his ear and he wanted to warn them that he was having an attack of some kind and that they should abort the landing and go round again to give them time to remove him from the pilot's seat, where he was swiftly becoming a danger to the safety of the aircraft. But he could say nothing at all because the pain had grown so great that it was blinding him, reducing his movements to spasms, paralyzing his throat and lungs so that he could make only soft, hollow animal sounds.

The rip in the aortic intima reached the junction with the

pericardial sac. There was a resistance there for a fraction of a second, and then the stress caused by the surge of arterial pressure tore the tough membrane and blood, fresh from the ventricle, spilled into the space between the pericardium and the heart itself. The result was a cardiac tamponade – the pressure building almost instantly in the interstice between heart muscle and pericardial sac. This had two results: it stopped the action of the heart and ripped away thousands of tiny arteries, veins, and ligaments on the surface of the heart. Ira Dayton was, to all intents and purposes, a dead man at that moment. But his dying came in a thrust of white-hot agony. He made a nasal, gasping sound in his spasming throat and pitched forward, arms stiffly out. His clutching insensate hands struck the control column with surprising force, catching Wingate by surprise.

These are the events that lead to the crash of Air Force One, thus observed from the ground:

The dignitaries and the news people, each from their particular vantage points, had watched the presidential plane approach the airport from the south. They had seen it cross the airport boundary and begin to flare for what appeared to be a routine landing. Now they were stunned to see the giant aircraft pitch forward at an altitude of no more than fifty to seventy-five feet. The angle of descent steepened to perhaps forty degrees, and the airplane struck the concrete runway nose first at a speed of one hundred and seventy-five knots. Later, witnesses would have conflicting stories about the crash of Air Force One. What actually happened would be lost in a welter of well-intentioned but hopelessly inaccurate and shocked reports from unqualified observers.

The last sentence leaves the reader with a feeling of comfortable superiority. Thanks to the author, he has become an insider, an accurate and qualified observer, completely familiar with the reasons for the crash. Yet as he reads through the first of the two extracts quoted above he will perhaps be obliged to confess some unfamiliarity with the medical and physiological terms awesomely paraded there: 'aortic intima', 'pericardial sac', 'ventricle', 'cardiac tamponade', etc. These are, to be sure, terms such as any medical college, or the nearest encyclopaedia, might supply, but they will have an evil look to the layman who finds them in his paperback as he sits packaged in the sky twenty-eight thousand feet over Greenland. What they spell out is catastrophe – the catastrophe that begins to overcome the doomed aircraft from the moment its flight begins. Colonel Dayton's heart condition becomes a metaphor expressing the decease of the plane; it is the inevitable event seen (indeed quite literally!) from the inside. Then the same event is presented as the happening that astonishes the outsiders, the people waiting on the tarmac. Now the technical vocabulary shifts into the ordinary register of aeronautical language: 'flare', 'pitch', 'altitude', 'angle of descent', 'runway', 'one hundred and seventy-five knots'. In this same technical register the disintegration of the aircraft is described:

> The airplane struck the runway, collapsing the nosewheel gear as though it were made of straws. The fuselage split aft of the flight deck, and the right wing broke away, spilling jet fuel over a wide area. The fuselage broke again at the wing root, and the tail tumbled to the right at an angle to the path of the disintegrating debris. Fire broke out only after the right engine disintegrated, but since the area and the tumbling wreckage had been liberally soaked with fuel, the fire was intense and widespread.

Compare this with the earlier description of Colonel Dayton's collapse:

> The rip in the aortic intima reached the junction with the pericardial sac. There was a resistance there for a fraction of a second, and then the stress caused by the surge of arterial pressure tore the tough membrane and blood, fresh from the ventricle, spilled into the space between the pericardium and the heart itself. The result was a cardiac tamponade – the pressure building almost instantly into the interstice between the heart muscle and the pericardial sac.

These are parallel events; they may even be regarded as the *same* event, viewed in different perspectives, and consequently in the vocabulary of different technologies. It is even possible to perceive lexical and syntactic correspondences between the two descriptive procedures, e.g.:

> The rip in the aortic intima reached the junction with the pericardial sac.

and

> The fuselage split aft at the flight deck.
> (Note 'rip' and 'split'.)

And again:

> . . . the stress caused by the surge of arterial pressure tore the tough membrane and blood, fresh from the ventricle, spilled into the space between the pericardium and the heart itself.

and

> . . . the right wing broke away, spilling jet fuel over a wide area.
> (Note 'tore' and 'broke away'; 'spilled' and 'spilling'.)

When close comparisons are made in this way, it is difficult to avoid the impression of a designed analogy between the man's body as it breaks down, spilling blood, and the aircraft's fuselage as it disintegrates, spilling fuel. The vocabulary of the two technologies, medicine and airframe construction, is thus put to imaginative purposes that transcend simple realism.

Every problem has a solution if it's big enough

The challenge to the technological imagination is a central feature of one of the actionbook's essential ingredients – the enormously insoluble problem that the hero will solve *because it's there*. There must be a fix, a tight corner, a nasty predicament from which he will extricate himself and his companions, if he has any. The old joke about cliff-hanger serials used to represent each instalment as beginning 'With one bound, Jack was free', because authors and script-writers hacking for an honest penny were not inclined to consider means of rescuing the hero from the mineshaft or the railway line where they last left him bound and gagged with a stick of dynamite and a merrily hissing fuse tucked into his back pocket. Modern writers of popular fiction cannot expect to evade their responsibilities in this way. The technology of escape has to be demonstrated; indeed there is a whole subgenre of actionbooks, the disaster story, which depends on the writer's power to explain in almost overwhelming detail how people solve impossible problems and overcome apparently unsurmountable difficulties.

Paul Gallico's *The Poseidon Adventure* is a good example of the disaster genre. It tells how a cruise liner, the *Poseidon*, is overturned by a giant wave and floats keel upward in the Atlantic while passengers who have survived the first impact of the catastrophe wander in darkness round the inverted mazes of the stricken ship, trying to find a way out. One party is led by a very remarkable Minister of the Gospel, a dynamic, squash-playing, loser-hating Princeton graduate and ex-gridiron star, the Reverend Dr Frank Scott. Scott's party painfully achieves the hazard-strewn ascent towards the keel, and comes at last to the engine room. Gallico describes at length and in considerable technical detail the sight that confronts the adventurers:

> The engine-room of a great quadruple-screw ocean liner consists of a series of platforms, some five decks high, connected by ladder-type stairs leading to open-work steel flooring or catwalks. These platforms are built around the huge central steam turbines and reduction gear housings. The auxiliary machinery, such as turbo generators, condensers, compressors, emergency compressors and a whole battery of pumps are (*sic*) ranged around the four sides, joined by what seems (*sic*) to be completely helter-skelter coils of pipes and wiring to feed steam under various degrees of pressure, oil, lubricating materials and electrical power.
>
> All this is attached to the double-bottomed fuel and ballast tanks which constitute the floor of the vessel, planned for maximum stresses of a forty-five degree roll. Crossbeams of heavy girders support the platforms, catwalks and conduits.
>
> When the *Poseidon* turned over, almost everything but the main propeller shafts was twisted, shaken, or torn away, either plummeting directly into the sea through the open well of the engine-room shaft, or tumbling down the sides in a cascade of tangled metal. Dynamos had plunged through their housings, shearing the steel as though it had been paper, leaving wedge or spear-shaped pieces, razor sharp, thrust upward in menacing pinnacles like miniature Dolomites.
>
> Mingled with these were curling sections of the platforms, reversed ladders with a half-dozen steps smashed out of their centres and the curved surfaces of the larger pipes, some of them crumpled, others cut open lengthwise, the way one slits a sausage skin. Everything was covered with a film of oil released from the bottom tanks when the heavy turbines had ripped loose from the floor plating.

At one point a giant reduction gear and its housing had broken away completely from its turbine unit, but instead of falling through to the sea, had been slammed against the sides of the engine-room by the centrifugal force of the capsizing and locked there, with the gear wheel jammed at an angle and held aloft by the crumpled housing. Scott's probing lantern showed up the square edges of the finely milled teeth curving outwards for several yards in an overhang, before receding into the general tangle of battered steel.

Fragments of this jumbled mountain reached to within a foot of the platform on which they had been resting. Their lights showed up a similar range across the stygian lake.

This long preamble establishes the problem. What follows presents the possibility of a solution:

Scott studied the outcroppings on the far side. Had he judged it an easier climb, he would have been prepared to have got himself and his party across the water. But it was, if anything, more formidable-looking and there was an overhang of metal pushed out at a thirty-degree angle, some eight feet from the edge which made it an impossible task.

Muller asked, "What are you looking for?"

Scott replied, "Path!" and then removing the light beam from across the lake, added, "Well, that leaves us no choice." He studied the precipice of metal on their own side.

Rogo said, "Where do you think you're going now?"

Scott replied simply, "Up there."

Shelby was horrified and cried, "Frank, you must be out of your mind! It's impossible. My family could never . . ."

The fanatic look was back in the Minister's eyes and his voice suddenly filled the vast cavern, "We're being tested. You believe in God; worship him by being worthy!"

The echo repeated, "Worthy" and died away. In a quite normal tone he said, "Don't think of it as you're seeing it, but simply as a mountain to be climbed. It's everything you find on a mountainside: crevices, projections, buttresses, pinnacles, clefts, foot and handholds. There's hardly a single peak left in the world that someone hasn't managed to climb."

Martin muttered under his breath, "Someone!" and Muller said "The Mount Poseidon Expedition."

"Exactly," Scott continued. "You've all seen photographs of mountain climbers roped together. The line is so arranged that the entire weight never falls upon one person, but is distributed. Is that clear? It's actually much simpler for us. We've only an ascent of fifty feet to make. There are . . ." he made a quick count as though he had forgotten – "thirteen of us. We'll all be double roped at say a distance of three or four feet apart."

The solution Dr Scott propounds is the practical application of a piece of lateral thinking: 'Don't think of it as you're seeing it, but simply as a mountain to be climbed.' The reader is not unprepared for this. Even as he describes the bizarre wreck of the engine room, the author produces an image that suggests mountaineering: 'thrust upward in menacing pinnacles like miniature Dolomites.' Other hints follow, words casually introduced, or so it seems at first, into the account of the great spillage of metal and machinery. There is an 'overhang', and then the piled-up wreckage is called a 'jumbled mountain'; a 'similar range' is glimpsed across the black pool of oily water – 'the stygian lake'. By the time Scott announces his solution, the answer is already there in the reader's mind; if we have been paying close attention, with the author and his hero, we will have effected the imaginative transformation of 'turbines', 'reduction gear housings', and 'reversed ladders' into 'crevices', 'projections', 'buttresses', 'pinnacles'. Here, as in the extracts quoted from Alfred Coppel's *34 East*, a shift of register in the vocabulary underlines the perceptual shift; in this instance, however, the perceptual shift is crucial to the solution of an apparently overwhelming problem. What others (Muller, Rogo, Shelby, Martin) cannot see, the actionbook hero (Scott) grasps immediately. He controls his destiny with his mental as well as his physical powers.

For such a man, however, it is necessary that the problem should be of respectable size. Little challenges will not do (the want of a safety-pin to keep up the heroine's shorts, the absence of the aspirin that might temporarily still a raging toothache) and in any case there is nothing to be done about them. Any problem can be solved if only it is big enough. The writer must accordingly work at the task of inventing the penultimate fix, the all-but-ineluctable snafu. Here Gallico works very hard indeed, patiently working from technical knowledge of what may ordinarily be found in a liner's engine-room, into an imaginative account of what that ordered world might look like if it were violently turned topsy-turvy, and so to the new and interesting image of fallen machinery as risen mountain. The gradual emergence of surreal or 'romantic' effects (like the glimpsing of the sinister 'range' on the far side of the 'stygian lake') depends on a welter of realistic detail, at its most profuse in the first paragraph of our extract. There we find a tumble of noun phrases ('turbo generators, condensers, compressors, emergency compressors, and a whole battery of pumps') in excited lists that twice lead the writer grammatically astray. (A plural verb, 'are', follows the grammatically singular subject, 'the auxiliary machinery', and the singular inflection of 'seems' is followed by a plural complement.) He also blends constructions that would have been better kept apart. Pipes feed steam, oil, and lubricating materials; wires feed electricity; but in the text 'pipes and wiring . . . feed steam under various degrees of pressure, oil, lubricating materials and electrical power'. This somewhat uncertain control of syntax is symptomatic of the overriding anxiety to impress with as many names as possible. The paragraph is not really an exposition; it is an inventory. Realism demands that the items in the inventory shall be correctly, or at least convincingly named, but it does not really matter if the reader does not know what a condenser might be or what a reduction gear housing might look like. It is enough for him to gather that such things are *complicating objects*; in this particular instance, large pieces of metal that would wreak grotesque havoc if airily detached from their customary seatings. This is the author's way of telling us that the problem is big enough for his hero to solve. It might be noted in passing that even in stories like *The Poseidon Adventure*, which are not exclusively masculine in orientation, but attempt to present some female characters and to give them equal weight with the men, the male is the dominant problem-solver. Only one of the problems confronting the *Poseidon* party is tackled by a woman. (Gallico rewards her with a fatal heart attack, even as the rescuers are going to work with the oxy-acetylene cutters.) Otherwise, resourceful response to a challenge is seen as the male prerogative. When Dr Scott falls to his death, after maniacally berating his Maker for bad sportsmanship, the conduct of the party, and the responsibility for solving further problems, with or without the collaboration of his companions, devolves upon another man, ostensibly the least likely candidate for the honours of captaincy, in the event an effective performer.

Stylistic types

Passages in which challenges are confronted and overcome are necessarily somewhat dense in stylistic texture, strenuous in diction, highly wrought in metaphor and image. The style is of an *intensive* type which, for the reader, may represent the true quality of the book, the showmanship that justifies the outlay of a few pounds or dollars. Clearly, however, it would be impossible (or if possible, a self-defeating achievement) to write a whole narrative at this level. In every actionbook there are gradations of style, as the tension of the story is raised or lowered, and in general there is an *extensive* style, a way of explaining and expounding, or simply of getting the actors from one big scene to the next, that sets the intensive passages into high relief, or even makes the base upon which they are built. The latter possibility is quite well illustrated by the *Poseidon* extract, in which the first paragraph is the extensive ground for the intensive elaboration that follows.

The extensive style includes dialogue, which, in these action narratives, is often used as a way of conveying factual information, supplying 'background', rehearsing personal histories, or outlining the circumstances of whatever position the actors find themselves in. Desmond Bagley's *Night of Error*, which offers, as its particular technological buzz, a knowledge of the chemical behaviour of manganese, contains many such passages of instructional dialogue, introduced by passages of flat reportorial prose. (This is perhaps appropriate to the character of the hero, a scientist no doubt accustomed to writing laboratory reports.) Thus the second section of the book's third chapter begins:

> We made a fair and untroubled crossing of the Atlantic. Geordie and Ian, together with the regular crew members, soon got the others into a good working pattern and spirits ran high. Kane, we were pleased to notice, fitted in well and seemed as willing and above-board as the others. Knowing that they were all curious as to our purpose I gave occasional rather deliberately boring lectures on oceanography, touching on a number of possible research subjects so that the matter of manganese nodules got lost in the general subject. Only two people retained an interest in what I had to say, and to them, in semi-private, I spoke at greater length about our quarry. One was Geordie, of course, and the other, not too

surprisingly and in fact to my satisfaction, was Bill Hunter. Already our diving expert, his interest and involvement might well be crucial.

This exordium is, in the narrator's own words, 'rather deliberately boring'. 'Rather', indeed, expresses the stylistic aim. The lexicon throughout is *downgraded* ('crucial' is the only word in the passage that suggests emotional strength), operating with the negative word-form ('untroubled') and the cliché-collocation ('spirits ran high', 'to my satisfaction', 'interest and involvement'). Even the sentence-structure avoids tension; the parentheses ('together with the regular crew members', 'we were pleased to notice', 'in semi-private', 'not too surprisingly and in fact to my satisfaction') wordily dispel any excitement that might be lurking in this ordinary account of a not-so-ordinary voyage. Then follows a dialogue:

> One afternoon they both joined me in the laboratory, at my request, to learn a little more. A quiet word from Geordie to Ian made sure we weren't going to be interrupted.
>
> Geordie picked up a nodule which I'd cut in half – I had brought a few on board to help my explanation along.
>
> He pointed to the white central core.
>
> "I suppose you'll tell me again that it's a shark's tooth in the middle of this rock. You never did get around to explaining that, did you?"
>
> I smiled and held up the stone. "That's right, it is."
>
> "You're kidding."
>
> "No I'm not – it happens often. You see, a shark dies and its body drifts down; the flesh rots or is eaten, the bones dissolve – what bones a shark has, it's cartilage really – and by the time anything reaches the very bottom there's nothing left but the teeth. They are made of sodium triphosphate and insoluble in water. There are probably millions of them on any ocean bottom.
>
> I opened a small box. "Look here," I said and gave him a larger white bone. It was as big as the palm of his hand and curiously convoluted.
>
> "What's this?"
>
> "It's a whale's earbone," said Bill, looking over his shoulder. "I've seen 'em before."
>
> "Right, Bill. Also made of sodium triphosphate. We some-

times find them at the core of larger nodules – but more often it's a shark's tooth and most frequently a bit of clay."

"So the manganese sticks to the tooth. How long does it take to make a nodule?" Geordie asked.

"Estimates vary from one millimetre each thousand years to one millimetre each million years. One chap estimated that it worked out to one layer of atoms a day – which makes it one of the slowest chemical reactions known. But I have my own ideas about that."

They both stared at me. "Do you mean that if you find a nodule with a half-diameter of ten millimetres formed round a tooth that the shark lived ten million years ago? Were there sharks then?" Georgie asked in fascination.

"Oh yes, the shark is one of our oldest inhabitants."

Conversations like this have all the tedium of loquacity and none of the pleasure of gossip; yet in books of this kind they occur regularly as a method of training the reader – who might otherwise prefer the fascination of watching paint dry – in the necessary scientific or technological attitudes. The dialogue is motivated, as far as the construction of the book is concerned, by the need to get these facts across at some point; the author uses a secondary character as a convenient feed-man whose business it is to prompt the narrator to tell him again what he and the narrator already know ('I suppose you'll tell me again . . .' etc.).

The dialogue is not really interactive, as the exchanges in women's magazine fiction might fairly claim to be, although the writer, by making occasional use of turnover sentences ('I smiled and held up the stone', 'They both stared at me'), or a reporting tag with an adverbial phrase ('Geordie asked in fascination'), or a participle clause ('said Bill, looking over his shoulder'), faintly simulates the concern of people engaged in a conversation that affects them personally. The devices that litter the presentation of dialogue in magazine fiction are here used sparingly or not at all. (There are no manner adverbs in this stretch of dialogue, and only one adverbial phrase of manner.) This is not dialogue in imitation of natural conversation; this is information in dialogue form, and the whole extract could in fact be rewritten as textbook prose without many changes in language beyond the writing in full of contracted forms ('It's'), the substitution of the formal word for the informal ('chap'), and the use of the passive or the existential sentence to cut out personal reference ('I have my own ideas about that'). Thus:

> When a shark dies, its body drifts downward through the water. As it sinks, the flesh rots or is eaten, and the bone, or rather the cartilage, dissolves. Only the teeth reach the bottom. They are made of sodium triphosphate and they are insoluble in water; millions of them are to be found, in all probability, on any ocean bed.
>
> The earbones of whales are also made of sodium triphosphate, and these, too are sometimes found at the core of larger manganese nodules; more often, however, it is a shark's tooth that is found, frequently attached to a piece of clay that has caused it to stick to a nodule. The nodules take a long time to form. Estimates vary from one millimetre every thousand years to one millimetre every million years. One researcher has estimated that the growth rate can be expressed as one layer of atoms a day. Were that the case, this would be one of the slowest chemical reactions known; however, it is a view not universally shared.

From some such understructure, not from the conception of personalities engaged in discussion, the dialogue is derived. The conversion into dialogue requires, of course, some rudimentary tact. This would hardly be convincing:

> "When a shark dies," I remarked, ruminatively scratching my left ear, "its body drifts downward through the water, if you see what I'm driving at. As it sinks, the flesh rots or is eaten, and the bone, or rather the cartilage, dissolves. Only the teeth reach the bottom." I paused to light my pipe.
>
> "Jeeze!" ejaculated Geordie, impressed.
>
> "They are made of sodium triphosphate," I resumed, smiling at Geordie's naïve wonderment, "and they are insoluble in water; millions of them are to be found, in all probability, on any ocean bed."
>
> "You mean . . .?" interjected Bill, questioningly.

This will not do simply because it strives too obviously to make an interaction out of a seminar paper. What Bagley has done in his own version amounts to a breakdown of the instructional text into dialogic form, with occasional stylistic touches to suggest conversational exchange.

At the climax of his story, Mr Bagley adds to the consequences

of human villainy the effect of natural violence, in the form of a
volcanic eruption:

And then Falcon blew.

There was a mighty roar as thousands of tons of water
exploded into superheated steam. A bright flickering glare
shone on us and the sunlight was dimmed as a pillar of steam
ascended into the sky.

The first wave reached us in less than fifteen seconds. As I
staggered, grabbing for support, I saw it racing down towards
Esmerelda, silhouetted against the raging furnace. It was a
monstrous wave, rearing mast high, creamed with dirty grey
spume and coming with the speed of an express train.

I crouched on the open deck, trying to flatten myself into
the planking.

The wave broke against *Esmerelda*. She heaved convulsively and ground against *Sirena*. There was a rending crash
and I thought that both ships must have been stove in. A flood
of near scalding water washed over the deck, and I writhed
as I felt the wound in my side.

Then the wave was past us and the ships dipped in the
afterwash, creaking and groaning in every timber. There were
four more huge waves, but none as high as the first. I staggered
to my feet, feeling the ships' curious writhing motion on the
water.

This represents, in the context of *Night of Error*, the 'intensive'
style that may be contrasted with the 'extensive' manner quoted
earlier. The object here is no longer to inform, expound, or ease
the continuity of the narrative, but to seize on the drama of the
intensely-experienced moment. It is achieved by putting the
lexicon strenuously to work. The verbs express dynamic
energy, violent, uncontrolled movement, disorientation, pain:
'exploded', 'staggered', 'grabbing', 'rearing', 'heaved', 'writhed',
'creaking', 'groaning', 'writhing'. Adjectives express intensity of
sensory quality, mass, or ferocity of aspect: 'superheated', 'bright
flickering', 'raging', 'monstrous', 'rending', 'scalding', 'huge'.
Several of the nouns – 'roar', 'glare', 'spume', 'speed', 'crash',
'flood', 'writhing' – register the perception of violent, agitated,
implicitly painful events. There is some use of figurative language, for instance 'creamed with dirty grey spume', 'coming
with the speed of an express train', 'the ships' curious writhing
on the water'. Non-human entities in several instances assume

the agent-role ('thousands of tons of water exploded into super-heated steam'; 'a bright flickering glare shone on us', 'a pillar of steam ascended into the sky', 'the first wave reached us . . .' etc.). If the language of this extract fails to engender real excitement, it is because much of its energy is the well-tried force of cliché: 'a mighty roar', 'the raging furnace', 'with the speed of an express train', 'heaved convulsively', 'a rending crash', 'creaking and groaning in every timber'. The clichés are nevertheless signals of authorial intention, notifications that we must now try to intensify our own responses to the narrative we have hitherto followed as obedient observers of accumulating detail.

The machoman's lexicon

It is in passages of intensive styling that the peculiar lexicon of the action narrative becomes most apparent. Here are the words that suit men's business – words with muscle, words with teeth, hard-knuckled words, levelled weapons of words, words to break your head rather than your heart, the machoman's lexicon. Random investigation of appropriate passages in a few novels yields the rather interesting result (no less interesting for being predictable) that verbs are emphatically macho, nouns and adjectives less so, adverbs barely at all. (It is hardly an extensive test, but a check through ten passages chosen from five novels – for each novel two passages of roughly a page in length – yielded only two examples of contextually highlighted manner adverbs.) This only serves to confirm the propriety of the description so often applied to these novels, 'action packed'. The packing of action or violent event into the verb is seen in the frequent occurrence of words denoting literal or psychological explosion: 'blow', 'blow up', 'detonate', 'explode', 'erupt'. There is a fairly large collection of verbs denoting movement plus speed, or movement plus sound, whether it be the sound of transit or the sound of impact: 'carom', 'clatter', 'hurtle', 'plummet', 'race', 'rattle', 'rumble', 'thud', 'wham', 'whip', 'whirr', 'whizz', 'zoom'. Also quite frequent are verbs expressing violent action upon surfaces or objects: 'fracture', 'grind', 'hammer', 'hurl', 'pound', 'slice', 'slit', 'snap', 'thrust', 'twist', 'wrench'. Other verbs denote impact, or a condition resulting from impact: 'crack', 'crash', 'crumple', 'shatter', 'skewer', 'splinter', 'tangle'. Still others relate to physical movements, gestures, involuntary utterances: 'gasp', 'groan', 'grunt', 'kick', 'lash (out)', 'pant', 'sprawl', 'whine'. A common feature of all these verbs is onomatopoeia; many are monosyllabic; some lend themselves readily to metaphoric transfer (for instance, bullets and machinery may 'whine' as well as humans; and in general these verbs may be governed by subjects denoting non-human as well as human agents).

Nouns and adjectives in this style are more or less satellites to the verb. (This may be putting the relationship the wrong way round, as some of the verbs are clearly denominal, e.g. 'plummet', 'hammer', 'skewer'; but the impression remains that the verb is the dynamic focus, so to speak.) Nouns like 'detonation', 'eruption', 'explosion', have verb-counterparts with which they alternate at stylistic need. Common occurrences are nouns literally or metaphorically indicative of violent disorder ('cascade', 'shambles', 'surge') or of physical pain ('agony', 'anguish', 'torture'). Nouns of the latter type often occur in context with words denoting emotional or pain-stricken utterance, e.g. 'outcry', 'scream', 'whine', or with others, like 'glare' and 'roar', suggesting oppressive visual or auditory sensation. Adjectives are comparably suggestive of violence, pain, discomfort, or bewilderment. There is an apparent liking, in dramatic representations of untoward events, for ' –ing' forms denoting processes of assault and breakage: 'grinding', 'rending', 'splintering', 'pounding'. Other common adjectives denote the results of assault or mishap: 'crippled', 'crumpled', 'jumbled', 'mangled', 'tangled', 'torn'. Some express unsettling movement – 'canting', 'swirling', 'whirling'; some, like 'appalling', 'sickening' are seemingly appropriate for general use in collocation with screams, thuds, crashes, noises, and various kinds of spectacle.

There is a short passage in Forsyth's *The Devil's Alternative* that usefully shows how verbs work in the macho lexicon and makes an incidental point about nouns. It reads as follows:

> He paused for a second as the passenger door was swung open, and died, the bullet from the hunting rifle skewering through his forehead, splintering the parietal bone and exiting through the rear of the cranium to lodge in an aide's shoulder.

This gruesome sentence at first appears to turn, in its gruesomeness, on the verbs 'skewering' and 'splintering'. But then that cold grey technical word 'exiting' takes on something of the same lurid colour; and the verbs generally are made to contrast horridly with cold grey technical nouns – the 'parietal bone' and the 'cranium'. It is the stylistic contrast between the macho verbs, 'skewering' and 'splintering' (meat is skewered, glass is splintered) and the scientific, emotionally neutral nouns, 'parietal bone', 'cranium', that endows this little passage with a peculiarly Forsythian flavour.

Man's business it may be, but on the whole it is rather nasty business, and the vocabulary of the actionbook tells us so in sentence after sentence. Even its outbreaks of decorative imagery imply violence and physical pain. 'The throwing knife', says Ian Fleming of one his omnicompetent killers, 'bloomed from the tips of his fingers like a white flame.' That is almost pretty, a multidirectional metaphor (knives bloom, flowers bloom, flames bloom, knives flame); but it does too much honour to an act of homicide. All this talk, all this vicarious enjoyment of destruction and suffering! The garrulous menace of maleness is not to be borne for long. Really, I am glad to be out of the blear and tousled line and back in my seat, with a dab of cologne on my forehead, a tomato juice in my hand, and in my ears, thanks to a two-dollar layout on earphones, the sound, slightly splintered, a little metallic, but still glorious and tender and manly, of the music of Johann Sebastian Bach. *Wachet auf!* Let us suck our jujubes and enjoy the chorale.

4 Beginnings, middles, and ends: some sample pieces

> To show our simple skill,
> That is the true beginning of our end.
> (The Artisans' Prologue, *A Midsummer Night's Dream*)

Or perhaps we should watch the in-flight movie? See, the stewardesses are putting up the screens, and although you and I are sitting at the very forward end of the non-smoking section, just by the galley, where that awful peripatetic bore in beach trousers has been loudly chatting up the girls for the last twenty minutes (his experiences in the Gulf, forsooth!) we can probably catch a fair glimpse of Robert de Niro, at least at half-length, if we lean sideways and look at the screen in the forward compartment. Or we could listen to the sound-track and try to guess at the pictures. Or maybe we should just shut our eyes, relax, and optimistically await the onset of sleep. They will bring us blankets, and little pillows that force a crick into your neck, and we can tilt our seats until the people behind start to buffet our backs, and we can put our seat lights out until the all-night accountant on your left insists on putting them on again. How does that sound? Let us drift, then, into reverie, lulled by drowsy tinklings from the galley, by distant rumours of the film that is just beginning, by the sense and nonsense of images taking smudgy shape behind our closed eyelids.

So much depends on the opening of a film; within minutes the watcher knows whether this fictive spectacle will hold his interest – but of course the same holds true of books and readers. There is probably no more crucial skill in the making of popular fiction than the art of opening; and there is perhaps no part of the composition in which authors attempt more variations on stereotyped patterns. Paperbacks need to be irresistible at the start. For women there may be a provocative glimpse of the heroine at the innocent beginning of her opulent romantic journey. Maybe skyscrapers tower above her as she makes her eager way through the canyons of downtown; or perhaps she is seen in her crisp white office blouse, prettily flustered as she drops an armful of files on the toes of Mr Robert, the junior partner; or perhaps, shielding her eyes from the fierce sun of the outback and peering moodily at the harsh brown vistas, she sighs, thinking of her sister Charlene who has gone to Sydney to be an opera singer. For men there will perhaps be a strange arrival on the Air France flight from Paris – a middle-aged librarian with a grizzled moustache and pebble-thick spectacles who slips into the Gents at Heathrow and re-emerges as a blue-eyed clean-shaven twenty-five-year-old baggage handler. Or there will be a single shot from a Smith and Wesson, drilling a neat round hole through the forehead of Roger Dubois, who will take no further part in the proceedings. Or there will be a description of a peaceful country town and a peaceful street where sheer horror is about to break in upon the peaceful house of a peaceful couple, their peaceful children, and their peaceful dog. Or perhaps there will be one of those vaguely symbolic preambles about fish, or reptiles, or rats repellently foraging by the light of a cold, forbidding moon. The types are predictable; the variations are endless. Here is Judith Krantz's opening to her 'glittering international tale' (as the cover blurb calls it) *Mistral's Daughter*:

> Fauve dashed through the lobby, her Stop-sign red slicker flapping around her, and managed to squeeze her way through the elevator doors a split second before they closed. Panting, she tried to furl her big striped umbrella so that it wouldn't drip on the other people who were jammed in with her, but, in the crowd, her arms were pinned to her sides.
>
> Earlier in the morning Fauve would have had the elevator pretty much to herself, but there hadn't been a single empty taxi in Manhattan on this rainy September morning in 1975. She'd had to wait endlessly for a bus on Madison Avenue and run the rest of the way across Fifty-seventh Street. Soaking and uncomfortable, she cautiously swivelled her neck around to survey the mob that hemmed her in. Would any of them get off before the tenth floor? No hope of that, she realized. The creaky, ancient elevator that rose so slowly in the Carnegie Hall office building was charged with a palpable cloud of tension and terror. Except for the operator, the small space

was packed with young women who were gripped in silent, fierce and frightened concentration. Each one of them had grown up knowing that she was, beyond any question, the most beautiful girl in her high school, in her hometown, in her state.

This elevator trip was the last step toward a goal they had been dreaming of feverishly for years. Before them lay an audition at the Lunel Agency, the most famous of all the modelling agencies in the world, the agency with the most prestige and the most power. Fauve felt the almost unbearable weight of the quivering anxiety and nervous anticipation that palpitated around her, and closing her eyes, she prayed for the ride to be over.

So here is Fauve, a wild thing, colourfully named daughter of a gusty artist called Mistral. The central character of the book is named in the book's first word. Lest we should miss her essential *fauvisme*, the writer gives her a red slicker and a big striped umbrella, and (a few lines after the extract cited above) speaks of 'the conflagration of Fauve's tumult of hair, of a red so extravagant that it could only be natural'. A little further on still, we discover that she is wearing 'kelly green tights . . . an orange turtleneck sweater and purple tweed trousers'. Thus we know the name, and something of the attached nature; we know the time of day (morning) and the weather (rainy); we know the place (Manhattan) and we even know the year (1975). This opening is really not so remote from the opening of a fairy tale. It provides the stock elements of name, location, time, and evaluation: 'Once upon a time there was a beautiful princess called Dulcibella who lived at the top of a mountain'; 'Back in 1975 there was a zany redhead called Fauve, who worked in Manhattan'. There is one unconventional touch, however; Judith Krantz invites her readers to make a false prediction about her heroine. Where is she going, this madcap who dashes and pants and prettily drips on people? Surely she is here on the same errand as the other girls scrimmaging in the elevator; she must be heading for an audition at the Lunel Agency, and of course she will get the job ('Interesting bones', murmured the photographer), and that will be her first step in a career which we shall follow with interest through all the vagaries of assignment and assignation. But we predict wrongly. Fauve works at the Lunel Agency. She has an office, and a secretary called Casey (who is

female, of course). Fauve's own surname is Lunel; her grandmother founded the agency. The sign on Fauve's office door
reads 'Director, Women's Division'; but we do not discover this
until the last line of the book's introductory section.

Perhaps not all readers will yield to this deception; but if it is
effective at all (as it is quite certainly intended to be), it is precisely
because Judith Krantz chooses to forgo the film-derived method
of opening, which presents without interpretative commentary
its sequence of images or actions, and instead resorts, after her
first paragraph, to explanatory comment not unlike the 'Dilations'
mentioned in connection with magazine fiction. (See p. 23.) The
grammatical symptoms of Dilation are evident in the recurrence
of 'had' and 'would': 'She'd had to wait endlessly for a bus on
Madison Avenue', 'Would any of them get off before the tenth
floor?', 'Each one of them had grown up knowing that she was,
beyond any question, the most beautiful girl in her high school,
in her hometown, in her state', 'This elevator trip was the last
step toward a goal they had been dreaming of feverishly for
years'. These dilative constructions are all assumed by the
unwary reader to apply to the one group of people; if 'She'd
had' applies to Fauve, then it is carelessly supposed that 'Each
one of them had' and 'They had' must also include Fauve.
The temporary deception is achieved not by 'filmic' means, but
through a little psychological game with the grammar of the text.

The beginning of John Gardner's *License Renewed* owes
much more to the conventions of cinematographic narrative:

The man who entered the airport washroom had light hair,
cut neatly to collar length. Stocky, and around five feet three
inches in height, he wore crumpled jeans, a T-shirt and sneakers. A trained observer would have particularly noted the
piercing light blue eyes, above which thin brows arched in
long curves that almost met above the slim nose.

The man's face was thin in comparison with his body, and
the complexion a shade dark in contrast to the colour of the
hair. He carried a small brown suitcase, and, on entering the
washroom, walked straight toward one of the cubicles, step-
ping carefully past a dungareed cleaner who was mopping
the tiled floor with a squeegee, though without enthusiasm.

Once inside, the man slid the bolt and placed the suitcase
on the lavatory seat, opening it to remove a mirror which he

hung on the door hook before starting to strip as far as his white undershorts.

To disrobe so thoroughly is excessively meticulous, we might think, even in the chaste washrooms of Dublin Airport. But alert readers are not taken in. They spot the clues: the small brown suitcase; the mere mention of sliding the bolt – for who, entering such premises on customary errands, does *not* slide the bolt, as a matter of course?; and finally the mirror, hung on the door hook. The veriest noddy of a reader can hardly escape the suspicion that this gentleman is about to transform his appearance, replacing those Identikit features – the *thin* brows arching in *long* curves almost meeting above the *slim* nose – with something altogether older and chubbier. Perhaps the noddy will not suspect that the 'dungareed cleaner' with his little zeugma ('mopping the tiled floor with a squeegee, though without enthusiasm') is an agent of MI5; that too, however, is a well-signalled clue. Everything is done in filmic style; the language 'focuses' on persons, objects, and actions (as a camera might zoom in on the hand sliding the bolt, or on the languid squeegee), and there is no interpretative comment at all. Explanations do not, in fact, begin until the second chapter, though we are allowed to believe implicitly, and correctly, as it happens, that the man in the toilet cubicle is up to no good.

Nor does the first chapter put a name to its central figure. Another fourteen pages must be turned before the tricky tenant of the bolted cubicle is identified as Franco, a wanted terrorist. The author does not take the option of immediately identifying his character: 'Franco headed for the airport toilet with his make-up bag. It had been a long flight.' Instead he chooses what might be called the definite/indefinite article opening, in which personages are at first not denominated but specified only with 'the' or 'a'. Some classic stories open in this way. *The Mayor of Casterbridge*, for example:

> One evening of late summer, before the nineteenth century had reached one-third of its span, a young man and a woman, the latter carrying a child, were approaching the large village of Weydon Priors, in Upper Wessex.
>
> . . . . . .
>
> The man was of fine figure, swarthy, and stern in aspect: and he showed in profile a facial angle so slightly inclined as to be almost perpendicular. He wore a short jacket of brown

corduroy, newer than the remainder of his suit, which was a fustian waistcoat with white horn buttons, breeches of the same, tanned leggings, and a straw hat overlaid with black glazed canvas.

This 'man' remains 'the man' for seven pages until he becomes 'Michael', and for a full sixteen pages until he is fully identified as 'Michael Henchard'. Hardy has his own good reasons for obliging his readers to pay attention to the actions of 'a man' who remains nameless until they, like the man himself, fully grasp the implications of what has occurred. (Henchard's full name is first announced in the solemn vow the man swears at the altar of a village church.) Hardy's descriptive technique, however, suggests the benevolent observer viewing at a distance people with whom he has yet to become acquainted; the artist, perhaps, showing figures in a landscape. John Gardner's, by contrast, suggests the police photographer, and the wording of his description owes something to the conventions of the police report: 'Stocky, and around five feet three inches in height, (wearing) crumpled jeans, a T-shirt and sneakers.' The detail of Hardy's description serves more than a picturesque purpose; it identifies his man as an agricultural labourer, a countryman in the decent garb of his kind. Mr Gardner's detail immediately suggests to the reader that his man is a suspect, a fugitive, perhaps a criminal. Readers understand this because they have heard so many police bulletins on the radio or in television broadcasts; the author communicates through covert appeal to our recognition of a familiar register.

Gardner's novel is an attempt to write a James Bond story in the style of the late Ian Fleming. His opening is certainly Flemingesque, but Fleming did not always resort to the acts-and-facts style at the beginning of a story. This is how *Diamonds are Forever* begins:

> With its two fighting claws held forward like a wrestler's arms the big *pandinus* scorpion emerged with a dry rustle from the finger-sized holes under the rock.
>
> There was a small patch of hard, flat earth outside the hole and the scorpion stood in the centre of this on the tips of its four pairs of legs, its nerves and muscles braced for a quick retreat and its senses questing for the minute vibrations which would decide its next move.
>
> The moonlight, glittering down through the great thorn

bush, threw sapphire lights off the hard, black polish of the six-inch body and glinted palely on the moist white sting which protruded from the last segment of the tail, now curved over parallel with the scorpion's flat back.

Slowly the sting slid home into its sheath and the nerves in the poison sac at its base relaxed. The scorpion had decided. Greed had won over fear.

Twelve inches away, at the bottom of a sharp slope of sand, the small beetle was concerned only with trudging on towards better pastures than he had found under the thorn bush, and the swift rush of the scorpion down the slope gave him no time to open his wings. The beetle's legs waved in protest as the sharp claw snapped round his body, and then the sting lanced into him from over the scorpion's head and immediately he was dead.

After it had killed the beetle the scorpion stood motionless for nearly five minutes. During this time it identified the nature of its prey and again tested the ground and the air for hostile vibrations. Reassured, its fighting claw withdrew from the half-severed beetle and its two small feeding pincers reached out and into the beetle's flesh. Then for an hour, and with extreme fastidiousness, the scorpion ate its victim.

All of Fleming's considerable relish for the nasty, his almost humorously precise passion for a good killing, is reflected in this opening. Once more we may be reminded of how some films open, with five minutes of dwelling on some savagely silent event in nature before the first pair of boots marches in, music blares over skittering tree tops and arid distances, and the titles begin to roll. Why does the director begin in this way? We assume a purpose, a figurative purpose, a moral purpose. So it is with Fleming's opening. The reader does not suppose that this is the introduction to an entomological treatise composed by an imaginative sadist. We take it that the scorpion and the beetle are engaged in some sort of representative or symbolic role-playing, and we anticipate, perhaps, some connection with the more or less voracious human personnel of the story which is to follow. Fleming's dispassionately objective pose, the stance of a man watching mere crawlies, is, after all, delusive. The scorpion is a lurking anthropomorph. It has psychological affects appropriate to man but not attestable in arachnids: 'Greed had won over fear.' It 'decides' things; it is capable of being 'reassured'; it even has table manners, eating 'with extreme fastidiousness'. (Later we are told how it 'slowly sucked the morsels of beetle flesh off its feeding pincers'; there's a good boy, then.) We have some reason to suppose that this horrid, clean-feeding scorpion prefigures a horrid clean-feeding human being, but if we were to make that supposition we would in fact be wrong. Fleming's preamble has no symbolic foreshadowings, makes no reference to any particular person or event, immediate or remote, in the narrative; all it appears to be saying is that this is a tough world of *sauve qui peut*, or scorpion eat beetle. When the scorpion itself meets death at the hands of a man wielding a stone, we are not surprised. We half expect the man in his turn to be killed by the pilot of the helicopter that presently whirrs into view ('it looked like a huge, badly-constructed insect') but that does not happen. The opening is not a pointer to anything in particular. It is a prose-poem celebrating the come-uppance awaiting types variously and inventively despatched by Fleming in his books: sundry members of the lower orders, communists, the deformed, and most males of non-European extraction. Fleming's nimble way with a plot incorporates a dismaying capacity for contempt and hatred; he despises blacks and orientals and he is not too fastidious about cleaning his pincers.

Pictures and conversations

But beginnings must yield to middles, and what we find in the middle of most paperbacks is an alternation of passages depicting persons, places, or events, and passages in which the depicted persons, or others, discuss matters relating to the depicted places and events; or, to use Alice's economical phrase, there are pictures and conversations. In women's magazine stories, the 'pictures' are rather brief patches (as we have called them; see p. 40) of narrative, yielding as quickly as possible to conversation. The principle of allowing dialogue to rule the action extends to paperback romances of the Mills & Boon type, although in these books the patches of relation, the 'pictures', may be somewhat longer than is possible in the tighter format of the magazine narrative. The following extract from Claudia Jameson's *Escape to Love* represents a typical pattern, indeed a typical configuration in narrative structure; a leading character is described, and the description is then followed by dialogue with a confronting character. First, then, the picture. Suzie is on holiday in Spain with her friend Harrie, a freelance journalist who has been granted an interview with an elusive grandee called Carlos Ferreira. When Harrie falls ill and is unable to keep her appointment, Suzie goes in her stead, using Harrie's name. (This subsequently presents her with two challenges: to account for the fact that a girl named Suzie goes around calling herself Harrie, and to explain how Harrie comes to be a girl's name in the first place. It is, incidentally, a minor creative principle in popular fiction that women of great spirit are called Chuck, Sam, Mickey, or – it has already been mentioned – Casey.) On arriving at Ferreira's house, Suzie is conducted by his servant Manolo to the great man's study. Her stomach tightens. She is ushered into the presence. The tableau follows:

> It was a large room. A study. The whole of one wall was covered with shelves of books from ceiling to floor. The rest of the walls were painted white to give an illusion of coolness. The floor, like the hallway, was covered in speckled, pale grey tiling and there were several expensive-looking rugs scattered about. On the right, stretching the whole length of the room and reaching from floor to ceiling, were windows, their shutters half closed against the light. It was very much a man's room. There was one black leather settee and three armchairs set out in a semi-circle, facing the window. And at the far end of the room, right in the centre, was an enormous leather-topped desk.
>
> Behind it sat Carlos Ferreira.
>
> Suzie and Manolo stood quietly, looking over at him. His head was bent in concentration as he continued writing in a large book spread out before him. It was as if he didn't even notice their presence, while his own presence dominated the entire room. Even as he sat, Suzie could see that he was very well built, and tall. She seemed unable to take her eyes from him. There was something – something almost magnetic about him, a sort of strength which emanated from him and reached her, despite the distance between them. This was, she acknowledged, a truly charismatic man, a man whose very presence commanded attention.

Here is a well-tried fictional stratagem; a man's general character is prefigured in the description of the room he lives or works in. There is evidence here of that solemn asseveration of the absurdly obvious which in magazine fiction is such a common symptom of the writer's anxiety to overlook no detail of social realism. 'Suzie and Manolo stood quietly, looking over at him.' But would Suzie and Manolo stand rowdily, looking out of the window? And 'he continued writing in a large book spread out before him'. How else could he write in it? Would he continue writing in a large closed book? What the author wants to convey is that when Suzie and Manolo entered, Ferreira was writing, and continued to write while they waited. Being quiet and 'looking over' at someone are typical bits of business for women and servants (the incessant energy of glances, grimaces, shrugs, and other physical activities for the heroine is discussed in Chapter 2); 'spread out before him' is realism in excess of realistic necessity, for the benefit of no one except those who need to be reminded that you cannot write in a book until you have opened it – or, as this piece of lexical upgrading puts it, 'spread it out'.

The semiotics of the passage are simple, and can be expressed in the formula *big room = big man; big man = big personality.* This of course does not follow at all, but it is the logic of romantic fiction; dynamic little chaps in poky offices littered with unpaid bills and superannuated whisky bottles belong to another kind of narrative, and Suzie would certainly not experience 'emanations' from a man with a small desk and cheap rugs. Size and scope are insistent themes in the vocabulary of the first paragraph: 'a large room', 'the whole of one wall', 'from ceiling to floor', 'The rest of the walls' (the author loses sight of the fact that there are only two walls remaining after she has accounted for the one covered with books and the one full of windows), 'stretching the whole length of the room', 'reaching from floor to ceiling', 'an enormous leather-topped desk'. We gather from this that the dimensions of the room and its furniture are large. Claudia Jameson operates the formula less happily in the next paragraph, which takes the step from big room to big man and big personality. The indications are vaguely impressive: he is 'very well built, and tall', his presence 'dominates' the room, there is 'something almost magnetic' about him, a 'sort of strength', which 'emanates' from him and reaches her 'despite the distance between them', he is 'truly charismatic', and his presence 'commands' attention.

So much for the picture. Now the first conversation between these people who are to become – our hot instincts tell us – will-bending, resistance-yielding romantic lovers:

Manolo moved further forward in an effort to catch his attention while Suzie stood, motionless, almost mesmerised.

"Senor?" Manolo said at length, and this was followed by a long sentence, none of which was understandable to Suzie apart from the mention of her name – or rather, Harrie's name.

As Manolo spoke Carlos Ferreira slowly raised his dark head, and cold, pitch black eyes fixed themselves on Suzie so rigidly and with such hostility that she wished the floor would open up and swallow her.

Manolo nodded politely to both of them and backed out of the room quickly, seeming pleased to get away, leaving Suzie standing there helplessly under that penetrating gaze. Carlos Ferreira was staring at her in much the same way that Manolo had stared, but from this man it was absolutely unnerving!

It seemed as if an eternity passed before he finally spoke, his voice deep, rugged, and authoritative. "And precisely who are you?" His eyes never moved from hers.

Suzie's mouth opened involuntarily and she stammered, shocked at his attitude, the open hostility. "Why, I – I'm . . . we have an appointment, *senor*. The – the interview."

"I asked you a question. Who are you?" he repeated. His command of English was obviously excellent, though heavily accented.

Suzie got the distinct impression that he was trying to contain anger – and not making a very good job of it. She had no idea what was upsetting him.

"I'm H-Harrie Patterson."

"Your name is Harriet, in fact?"

"N-no, just Harrie. I – you – – you gave me an appointment. We – you were expecting me today. I . . ." Aware that she sounded as nervous as she felt, her voice trailed away, her heart sinking with sudden foreboding that she was in for a very difficult morning.

Senor Ferreira didn't speak. There was no flicker of recognition in the cold eyes, so Suzie went on to tell him of the time of their appointment and of the magazine she was working for. There was a long and nerve-racking silence. She began to think that Harrie had made some dreadful mistake . . . got her dates mixed up, perhaps, or . . .

"Sit down!" The powerful voice cracked like a whip.

Thankfully, Suzie sank into the nearest chair, her hands

trembling as she put her bag and the tape recorder on the floor beside her.

After the emanations, the eye-contact: the 'cold, pitch black eyes' 'fix themselves' on her. Then comes the voice, 'deep, rugged, and authoritative', and also 'powerful', '(cracking) like a whip'. The tags and inserts of the dialogue sustain the theme of power already established in the depiction of the study. It is not a conversation in which the participants support each other, passing the conversational initiative back and forth. He challenges, she defends or evades. His first word to his future wife is a co-ordinating conjunction (as though their squabble had already begun, elsewhere), and of his four utterances in this first piece of dialogue, three are questions, two are commands. Of Suzie's three answers, two are incomplete. And she stammers. In short, the conversation fulfils the expectations raised by the introductory picture, of male dominance and timid female submission. Immediately there follows another picture, a closer description of Carlos Ferreira's appearance, which precedes a further section of conversation.

This pattern of writing, which might be called the 'character and follow-up' procedure, is common in paperback romances. It also occurs in more elaborate and varied forms in fiction with slightly higher literary pretensions. The general principle is that the conversation is in some way 'keyed' by the preceding picture, whether the portrayal is of a person or of a scene. In magazines and in paperbacks of the Mills & Boon type, dialogue is the customary mode of narration and the pictorial or descriptive element is a secondary feature, perhaps most evident when, as in the extract quoted above, a major character is introduced. However, as it is necessary to make transitions from dialogue to dialogue, the common structure of paperback romance can be described as an alternating series of small pictures and long conversations.

Thriller fiction also exploits linkages and juxtapositions of description and dialogue; not so much, perhaps, in the 'character and follow-up' procedure (though that occurs), as in dramatic sequences of scene and enactment. Here is an instance from Robert Ludlum's *The Parsifal Mosaic*, a book incorporating what *The Los Angeles Times* calls 'an abundance of fast and usually violent action described with great immediacy'. In this extract the 'immediacy' of violence requires the 'intermediacy' of a brooding descriptiveness. Thus the passage (it is the opening of a chapter) begins:

> The man in the dark overcoat and low-brimmed hat that shadowed his face climbed out of the two-toned coupe; with difficulty he avoided stepping into a wide puddle by the driver's door. The sounds of the night rain were everywhere, pinging off the hood and splattering against the glass of the windshield, thumping the vinyl roof and erupting in the myriad pools that had formed throughout the deserted parking area on the banks of the Potomac River. The man reached into his pocket, took out a gold-plated butane lighter and ignited it. No sooner had the flame erupted than he extinguished it; replacing the lighter in his pocket, he kept his gloved hand there. He walked to the railing and looked down at the wet foliage and the border of thick mud that disappeared into the black flowing water. He raised his head and scanned the opposite shoreline; the lights of Washington flickered in the downpour. Hearing the footsteps behind him, leather scraping over the soaked gravel, he turned.

No doubt the most striking feature of this paragraph is the presence, in some strength, of the machoman's lexicon. What is the substance of this description? Only that on a very rainy night a man emerges from a (stylish and presumably expensive) car, produces from his pocket a (presumably costly) lighter, strikes it, douses it, and waits, peering into the downpour. The content of the description is dull, to say the least of it; it is the lexicon that sets up expectations of imminent mayhem. The rain itself is a hooligan – 'pinging' off the hood, 'splattering' against the windshield, 'thumping' the roof of the car, 'erupting' in puddles. (This is upgrading with a vengeance; and 'erupt', in any case, surely involves a rising from within, not a descent from without.) When the lighter is 'ignited', its flame also 'erupts', until it is 'extinguished'. Ostensibly the theme of the description is the excessive bleakness of a miserably wet night (and what is a well-to-do fellow who owns a two-tone coupe and a gold plated lighter doing in a place like this, on a night like this?); implicitly, the promise of the description is battery, bullets, and the thud of falling bodies. Another important stylistic feature is the definite/indefinite technique of exposition. We know that the location is Washington, by the banks of the Potomac River; otherwise there are no names. Rather, there is the definite article:

the man
the dark overcoat and low-brimmed hat that shadowed his
face

the two-toned coupe
the driver's door
the sounds of the night
the hood
the glass of the windshield
the vinyl roof
the myriad pools that etc.
the deserted parking area etc.
the banks of the Potomac River
the flame
the lighter
the railing
the wet foliage
the border of thick black mud etc.
the black flowing water
the opposite shoreline
the lights of Washington
the downpour
the footsteps
the soaked gravel

Twenty-two instances are listed here, from a passage of text
consisting of seven (typographically defined) sentences. By contrast, the passage underplays the indefinite article or other forms
of deixis: 'a wide puddle', 'a gold-plated butane lighter', 'his
face', 'his gloved hand', 'his pocket', 'his head'. Here and there
the definite article marks the progression of a syntactic series
that gradually narrows the descriptive specification: 'erupting in
the myriad pools that had formed throughout *the* deserted parking area on *the* banks of *the* Potomac river.' The actor and the
occasion are undefined, but the scene itself crackles and sputters
with definition. The most remarkable instance is perhaps in the
last sentence of the paragraph, beginning 'Hearing the footsteps
behind him . . .'. One might expect, simply, 'Hearing footsteps';
the article conveys the impression that the footsteps, too, are
specifically appropriate to the scene, and that the advent of the
footstep-maker is expected. The newcomer is described thus:

A man approached, coming into view through blocks of darkness. He wore a canvas poncho printed with the erratic shapes

of green and black that denoted military issue. On his head was a heavy wide-brimmed leather hat, a cross between a Safari and a Digger. The face beneath the hat was thirtyish, hard, with a stubble of a beard and dull eyes set far apart, which could barely be seen between the squinting flesh. He had been drinking; the grin that followed recognition was as grotesque as the rest of him.

In these five sentences, the role of the articles is of some interest. The first three are framed predominantly round nominal phrases with the indefinite article or no article at all. (The exceptions are 'his head' and 'the erratic shapes that . . .' etc.):

a man
blocks of darkness
a canvas poncho
a heavy wide-brimmed leather hat
a cross between a Safari and a Digger

The last two sentences re-establish the specifying role of the definite article, for while the indefinite description continues in the fourth sentence – 'with a stubble of a beard and dull eyes set far apart' – key descriptive phrases are marked with 'the':

the face beneath the hat
the squinting flesh
the grin that followed recognition
the rest of him

He has become *the man*, and takes his place on the scene beside the other man. At the beginning of the dialogue which now follows, the speech-reporting tags show how the man talks to the man:

"Hey, how about it, *huh!*" cried the man in the poncho, his speech guttural, slurred. "*Wham!* Splat! Boom! . . . *kaboom!* Like a fuckin' gook rickyshaw hit by a tank. *Wham!* You never seen nothin' like it!"

"Very fine work," said the man in the overcoat.

"You betch-er ass! I caught 'em at the pass, and *kaboom!* Hey, I can't hardly see you. It *is* you, ain't it?

"Yes, but you disappoint me."

"Why? I did good!"

"You've been drinking. I thought we agreed you wouldn't."

"A couple of balls, that's all. In my room, not at no gin mill
. . . no sir!"

"Did you talk with anyone?"

"Christ, *no!*"

"How did you get out here?"

"Like you said. On a bus . . . three buses . . . and I walked
the last couple of miles."

"In the road?"

"*Off* it. Way off, like it was an S and D in Danang."

"Good. You've earned your R and R."

"Hey, Major . . .? Sorry, I mean . . . sir."

"What is it?"

"How come there was nothin' in the papers? I mean it was
one big blow! Musta burned for hours, seen for a couple of
miles. How come?"

"They weren't important, Sergeant. They were only what I
told you they were. Bad men who betrayed people like you
and me, who stayed over here and let us get killed."

"Yeah, well, I evened a few scores. I guess I should go back
now, huh? To the hospital."

"You don't have to." The civilian who had been addressed
as "Major" calmly took his gloved hand out of his pocket. In
it was a .22-caliber automatic, concealed by the darkness and
the rain. He raised it at his side and fired once.

The man fell, his bleeding head sinking into the wet poncho.
The civilian stepped forward, wiping the weapon against the
cloth of his overcoat. He knelt down and spread the fingers
of the dead man's right hand.

The episode thus completed represents a quite common
scheme of construction in which Description or Commentary is
followed by Dialogue which is rounded off by further Description
or Commentary. (It happens to be the compositional pattern of
the first chapter of *Pride and Prejudice*, a work otherwise remote
in manner and content from the fictional domains presided over
by Mr Ludlum.) The value of this construction is that when
description and dialogue are read in tandem each element is
seen to contribute pieces of a solution to the teasing puzzle of
identities and circumstances which the thriller writer offers for
our entertainment. In this case we observe how 'the man in the
dark overcoat' becomes 'the civilian who had been addressed
as "Major" ', and how 'a man' becomes 'the man in the poncho',

who is addressed as 'Sergeant' and acquires the ultimate, dismissive identity of 'the dead man'. From these clues we may at least infer that the two men are ex-military personnel (their conversation confirms this), and that one of them has some wealth and status while the other is down on his luck. (The 'civilian' has a 'dark overcoat' to go with his gold-plated lighter and his two-tone car; the 'Sergeant' has only a 'wet poncho'.) Long before the murderous final act of this mini-drama we have assumed, without benefit of interpretative comment, that in one case 'the man' is a somebody, with power and influence, while in the other 'the man' is a nobody, a vulnerable derelict and dupe.

Similarly, when the dialogue with its descriptive prelude and conclusion are attentively read in relationship to each other, it becomes clear that certain apparently casual or insignificant details are 'plants', small items of information that will provide explanatory references for subsequent events. The first paragraph tells us that after 'the man' put his lighter back into his pocket 'he kept his gloved hand there'. The closing description repeats the phrase 'his gloved hand'; we now know why it is gloved, and why he has kept it in his pocket. But why does not the Sergeant – a combat veteran, after all – see the weapon when the 'Major' produces it, at least for long enough to attempt some kind of response? The immediate answer is that the gun is 'concealed by the darkness and the rain' – that torrential rain that has been 'erupting in the myriad pools' since the first paragraph, those 'blocks of darkness' that figure in the second. The Sergeant's eyes, besides, are 'dull', and the author is obliged to draw our attention, in a remarkable phrase, to 'the squinting flesh'. The Sergeant himself, drunk or myopic or both, comments 'Hey, I can't hardly see you'. He cannot see the weapon, or how it is angled to shoot him in the head ('his bleeding head sinking into the wet poncho'), so that the appearance of a suicide may be contrived. But would not a gun, even a .22, make a noise? Look again at the first paragraph, where the rain 'pings' and 'splatters' and 'thumps', presumably drowning out other reports and percussions. The author has anticipated our objection. Look at the pictures, listen to the conversation, and piece the story together, if you can.

The dialogue itself is remarkable for the absence of any interpretative comment, apart from the reporting tags in the first exchange ('cried the man in the poncho, his speech guttural, slurred'; 'said the man in the overcoat'). Information about the attitudes and personalities of the two participants is conveyed by the mimicry of speech-style and social dialect. Whereas Claudia Jameson can only tell us, of her magnetic Spanish grandee, that 'his command of English was obviously excellent, though heavily accented', Robert Ludlum is at pains to document the various emphases and inflections of his semi-literate Vietnam veteran, obscenities and all. The Sergeant's language, like his dress and general appearance, makes him more prominent in the dialogue than his partner, the 'Major', whose speech is as discreet and unremarkably correct as his dark overcoat. The Sergeant's foul-mouthed whoops and ungrammatical mumblings only serve to emphasize his role as a sadly corrupted and corruptible monster, a conveniently dispensable piece of human wreckage. The 'Major''s speech, though less colourful, less demonstrative of a character, is in a way more subtle. His careful questioning of the Sergeant has a double discursive function. It is both plot-orientated and reader-orientated. It represents the 'Major''s concern to satisfy himself that the Sergeant has followed instructions. (What these have been, we infer from the text; no one supposes that when the civilian asks 'How did you get out here?' he is looking for information about public transport.) At the same time it tells the reader something about the 'Major' and his manipulative, puppeteering relationship with the Sergeant.

There are descriptive bases, so to speak, pictorial episodes significantly juxtaposed with blocks of dialogue. The dialogue is either a form of commentary on the description, as in the example quoted above, or in some cases the change in narrative mode (from description to dialogue) may represent a total shift of scene and reference. This happens not infrequently in books with multiple plots, several strands of narrative, and diverse locations of simultaneous action. (While the Cabinet assembles in London, an unidentified man with a tattoo on his left clavicle has just been pushed under a train in Rome, and two dissidents are waiting anxiously in a farmhouse near the East German border; this not implausible sequence might be realized in the form Dialogue – Description – Dialogue.) It is comparatively rare for dialogue to be compositionally idle, representing nothing more than small talk or phatic communion – though Ian Fleming, for example, will occasionally negotiate a turn in the narrative by inserting a little dialogue about local customs or food and drink. Thus in *Diamonds are Forever*:

There was a medium dry Martini with a piece of lemon peel waiting for him. Bond smiled at Leiter's memory and tasted it. It was excellent, but he didn't recognize the Vermouth.

"Made with Cresta Blanca," explained Leiter. "New domestic brand from California. Like it?"

"Best Vermouth I ever tasted."

"And I've taken a chance and ordered you smoked salmon and Brizzola," said Leiter. "They've got some of the finest meat in America here, and Brizzola's the best cut of that. Beef, straight-cut across the bone. Roast and then broiled. Suit you?"

"Anything you say," said Bond. "We've eaten enough meals together to know each other's tastes."

"I've told them not to hurry," said Leiter. He rapped on the table with his hook. "We'll have another Martini first and while you drink it you'd better come clean." There was warmth in his smile, but his eyes were watching Bond. "Just tell me one thing. What business have you with my old friend Shady Tree?" He gave his order to the waiter and sat forward in his chair and waited.

Fleming's food-snobbery (really not so much a snobbery as a form of gastronomical one-upmanship) is well known. He appears to attach some importance to meals as likely markers of significant developments in the action – in one of his tales our hero is almost blown up at breakfast time while he ingests half a pint of orange juice, three eggs, lightly scrambled, with bacon, toast, marmalade, and a double portion of café Espresso with cream. In the present instance, however, the occasion and the dialogue represent no function in the narrative other than that of supplying a transition.

It is more usual for dialogues to fall into one or other of three categories, all related to the progress of the narrative and the furnishing of information to the reader. One of these types is *confrontational*, and includes challenges, quarrels, disputes, interviews, and any kind of personal encounter in which the participants are in overt or covert opposition to each other. The dialogue of Suzie and Carlos is of this kind; so, in its own way, is that of the 'Major' and the Sergeant. Another type is *instructional*. Here the whole purpose of the dialogue is to convey information – ostensibly from one character to another, but ultimately from author to reader – about matters of science, technology, politics, world events, etc., some knowledge of which is essential to the understanding of the plot. The extract quoted in Chapter 3, p. 74, from Bagley's *Night of Error*, represents the type. The third category is that of *collaborative* dialogue, in which the interactants are made to support each other in building up a series of exchanges which cumulatively present, for the reader's benefit, a picture of events, histories, personalities, and relationships. Collaborative dialogue is often an alternative to descriptive summary, including the recounting of past events. The following extract from Wilbur Smith's *Eagle in the Sky* records a part of an episode in which the central characters meet for the first time. David (the hero of the book) is attracted to Debra, but is jealous of her companion, Joe, not realizing that Joe is Debra's brother. Their car, 'a battered old CV.100', has been destroyed, and he is about to give them a lift in his own car, a Mustang. Debra is impressed by David's evident affluence:

With one sweeping glance, she assessed the Mustang and its contents. David watched her check the expensive luggage, the Nikon camera and Zeiss binoculars in the glove compartment and the cashmere jacket thrown over the seat. Then she glanced sideways at him, seeming to notice for the first time the raw silk shirt with the slim gold Piaget under the cuff.

"Blessed are the poor," she murmured, "but still it must be pleasant to be rich."

David enjoyed that. He wanted her to be impressed, he wanted her to make a few comparisons between himself and the big muscular buck in the back seat.

"Let's go to Barcelona," he laughed.

David drove quietly through the outskirts of the town, and Debra looked over her shoulder at Joe.

"Are you comfortable?" she asked, in the guttural language she had used before.

"If he's not – he can run behind," David told her in the same language, and she gawked at him a moment in surprise before she let out a small exclamation of pleasure.

"Hey! You speak Hebrew!"

"Not very well," David admitted. "I've forgotten most of it," and he had a vivid picture of himself as a ten-year-old, wrestling unhappily with a strange and mysterious language with back-to-front writing, an alphabet that was squiggly tadpoles, and in which most sounds were made in the back of the throat, like gargling.

"Are you Jewish?" she asked, turning in the seat to confront him. She was no longer smiling; the question was clearly of significance to her.

David shook his head. "No," he laughed at the notion. "I'm a half-convinced non-practising monotheist, raised and reared in the Protestant Christian tradition."

"Then why did you learn Hebrew?"

"My mother wanted it," David explained, and felt again the stab of an old guilt. "She was killed when I was still a kid. I just let it drop. It didn't seem important after she had gone."

"Your mother – " Debra insisted, leaning towards him, " – she was Jewish?"

"Yeah. Sure," David agreed. "But my father was a Protestant. There was all sorts of hell when Dad married her. Everyone was against it – but they went ahead and did it anyway."

Debra turned in the seat to Joe. "Did you hear that – he's one of us."

"Oh, come on!" David protested, still laughing.

"Mazaltov," said Joe. "Come and see us in Jerusalem some time."

"You're Israeli?" David asked, with new interest.

"Sabras, both of us," said Debra, with a note of pride and deep satisfaction. "We are only on holiday here."

Much of this dialogue might have been written as continuous prose – as 'Dilation' – since what it conveys, in the main, is some hitherto undivulged information about David's personal history. His Jewishness – or his 'right of return', as Debra puts it – has to be established as an auxiliary motive for pursuing Debra back to Israel and joining the Israeli air force. That this passage is set in dialogue is mainly a matter of compositional rhythm, in the alternations of picture and conversation. The preceding pages have been generally descriptive, and have included brief pen-portraits of Debra and Joe. Now the principals have met, it is reasonable that their meeting should be recorded in dialogue, even though the function of the dialogue is to parcel out information, some of which, one might think, would not be naturally or easily divulged to a new acquaintance in the first five minutes of serious conversation. The essentially collabor ative nature of this dialogue is reflected in some of the speech-reporting tags: 'she asked', 'David explained', 'Debra insisted', 'David agreed'. Debra conscientiously elicits the information that David obligingly supplies; they work together to tell the reader the story. David's willingness to play the dialogic game sometimes transcends conversational likelihood, as when he laughingly dismisses himself as 'a half-convinced non-practising monotheist, raised and reared in the Protestant Christian tradition'. Perhaps this is such a gobbet of speech as one might produce naturally, between gear-changes, but it looks a good deal like an authorial attempt to gabble through some outstanding details of his hero's personal dossier. It sometimes appears that dialogue is a useful catch-all for scraps of incidental information.

And some were more or less happy for the next two weeks

But the last page must come, when there is no more information to be given, only some form of leavetaking – 'a sense of ending', it has been called – to be demonstrated. The act of ending is as a rule quite short in comparison with the process of beginning. It may be as short as three brief sentences:

> I rode down to the street floor and went out on the steps of the City Hall. It was a cool day and very clear. You could see a long way – but not as far as Velma had gone.

Velma is a murderess who has committed suicide; the book is Raymond Chandler's classic *Farewell, My Lovely*. Here the sense of ending is contained in the imagery of departure ('I rode down to the street floor and went out') and prospect ('you could see a long way'); 'out', 'long', 'way', and 'far' are in themselves virtual tokens of conclusion. The implication of putting past experience behind and turning elsewhere, the note of 'fresh woods and pastures new', the suggestion of a journey in prospect, of living happily ever after, or at least of living to fight another day, occur frequently. Thus Hammond Innes's narrator, at the end of *Levkas Man*:

> Later, much later, the dawn broke, spilling pink across the sky. I was on deck then, tired and bleary-eyed with lack of sleep, watching the last of Greece faded away astern, the

mountains of Cephalonia a dark cloud-capped rampart low on the horizon. The sea was flat calm, no breath of wind touching the surface, and there was no ship anywhere in sight. I watched as the clouds were edged with gold and the sun rose above them, a great burning orb, and then I swung the wheel over and turned the bows to the south.

Again the writing turns on notions of departure from the old ('the last of Greece', 'away astern', 'low on the horizon') and the prospect of the new ('swung the wheel *over* and turned the bows *to the south*'). There is something else, however, an ima-gery of benediction as the clouds in that low, dark rampart are 'edged with gold' when the sun rises 'above them'. The sunrise becomes a symbol both of conciliatory farewell to the past and hopeful salutation of a new day.

Another feature common to these two endings is the solitude of the narrator, implicit in Chandler, emphasized by Innes, whose hero, even at the end of the book, needs to slip away quietly because he is a wanted man in Greece. (Hence 'The sea was flat calm, no breath of wind touching the surface and *there was no ship anywhere in sight*'.) This note of solitude is also apparent in the final paragraph of Frederick Forsyth's *The Day of the Jackal*. 'The Jackal', a hired assassin who throughout the book is desperately hunted by the French police, has been killed in the very act of trying to assassinate General de Gaulle. The policeman who has pursued and finally killed him attends his burial:

The following day the body of a man was buried in an unmarked grave at a suburban cemetery in Paris. The death certificate showed the body to be that of an unnamed foreign tourist, killed on Sunday August 25th, 1963, in a hit-and-run accident on the motorway outside the city. Present was a priest, a policeman, a registrar and two grave-diggers. Nobody present showed any interest as the plain deal coffin was low-ered into the grave, except the single other person who attended. When it was all over he turned round, declined to give his name, and walked back down the cemetery path, a solitary little figure, to return home to his wife and children.
The day of the Jackal was over.

It is not explicitly stated that the 'single other person', the 'solitary little figure' is the Jackal's antagonist, Commissaire Claude

Lebel. We are left to infer it; Forsyth, so prodigal of names, so dependent on them for stylistic effect, signals the end of his narrative with a retreat into namelessness. He retains, however, his passion for facts and figures, including dates, and in that respect the end of the story is reminiscently tied to the opening, which also notes a date:

> It is cold at six-forty in the morning of a March day in Paris, and seems even colder when a man is about to be executed by firing squad. At that hour on 11th March 1963, in the main courtyard of the Fort d'Ivry, a French Air Force colonel stood before a stake driven into the chilly gravel as his hands were bound behind the post, and stared with slowly diminishing disbelief at the squad of soldiers facing him twenty metres away.

This briskly competent opening (which somewhat resembles the beginning of Ambrose Bierce's *An Occurrence at Owl Creek Bridge*) is written with Mr Forsyth's customary relish for numerical detail: it is six-forty in the morning (a lesser practitioner would have made it six-thirty), and the firing squad stands twenty metres away from the condemned man. The really significant numeral, however, is the date, 11th March 1963, marking one of the termini of the period called in the book's title and in its final line, 'the day of the Jackal'. The other terminus is the date given in the final paragraph, August 25th 1963. The ending of Forsyth's book refers us to its opening, not only this specific detail, but also in the general nature of the scenes depicted; both show bleak locations, and both represent the failure and solitary death or burial of a would-be assassin.

Shadows of regret and doubt, intimations of uncertainty, bleak acceptances of life for what it is, sometimes trouble the endings of male-orientated stories. James Bond, it is true, is never less than buoyantly macho and lightly libidinous after his encounters with monsters, madmen, mutants, and murderous machinery, but other heroes depart from their stories as sadder and wiser men. The woman's romance, by contrast, regularly ends with a confident promise – sealed with a kiss or something even more friendly – of a glittering and shadowless future. Here is Barbara Cartland, all amorous guns blazing, at the end of her historical romance *The Naked Battle*:

> And as he kissed her, as his lips pressed themselves against

her mouth, her eyes, her cheeks and the softness of her neck, Lucilla felt a fire rise within her ignited, she knew, by the fire in him.

"I love . . . you . . ." she tried to say but her voice was deep and passionate and seemed almost to be strangled in her throat.

"You are mine!" Don Carlos cried. "Mine completely and absolutely."

He kissed her again until she felt the world disappear and once again they were on a secret island of their own surrounded by a boundless sea.

It was what she had felt when she was with him in the little Pavilion; but now it was more real, more wonderful, more intense.

Ever since she had known him she had changed and become alive to new possibilities within herself.

Now she knew she could never go back to what she was before, because she had been reborn! Reborn to a new life and above all to love.

It was a love that was perfect, and Divine, a love that was not only of the body but of the soul and the spirit.

"I love you! Oh, Carlos . . . I love you with . . . all of me!" she whispered.

He took the last words from her lips saying fiercely:

"You are mine, my beautiful, adorable wife, now and for all eternity!"

This is not without its ardent moments of unintended humour. Don Carlos ('You are mine! Mine completely and absolutely') sounds like a man gratefully retrieving his PhD thesis from the railway lost property office. In the milder context of sexual relationships it might be thought that he comes on a little strong. Humour apart, it is just this note of irresistible conquest and unresisting surrender that characterizes the endings of countless romances by Ms Cartland and others. Conquest and surrender, however, are sanctioned by a spirituality that turns an earthly embrace into an act of divine union. Lucilla's utterances may be 'passionate' and 'strangled', her sensations 'more real', 'more wonderful', 'more intense', but she communes with herself in the language of religion: she is 'reborn' to a love that is 'perfect, and Divine', a love 'not only of the body but of the soul and spirit'. If ever there was a case of having your sex and sublimating it, it is here. Lucilla bids farewell to the past in the characteristic grammar ('had' + modals) of the 'dilative' style:

> Ever since she had known him she had changed and become alive to new possibilities within herself.
>
> Now she knew she could never go back to what she was before, because she had been reborn!

While Don Carlos, with characteristic enthusiasm and hyperbole, looks forward to the years ahead:

> "You are mine, my beautiful, adorable wife, now and for all eternity!"

And thus, in each case, the process of sentimental education ends in exclamation marks.

Anne Weal's *Bed of Roses*, a Mills & Boon romance, also ends with the conciliatory embrace of joyfully enlightened lovers. Coming Home, that necessary process discussed in Chapter 2, here extends into Going To Bed. Annis and Drogo, the happy pair, have made their final explanations. It only remains for Annis to speak:

> "So now there are no more barriers to our understanding of each other. You have my heart and I, unbelievably, have yours," she said happily.
>
> As she spoke she slipped one hand inside the red silk of his robe and placed it over his heart. "You feel as warm and solid as a rock which has had the sun on it."
>
> His serious look lightened. Smiling, he copied her gesture.
>
> "And you feel as soft as a dove."
>
> "You can't feel my heart beating there."
>
> "No, but I can feel mine."
>
> So could she. Suddenly, against her palm she could feel the throbbing of a strong, accelerated heartbeat as his ardour revived and ignited the flame in his eyes.
>
> As she swayed towards him, her breathing quickening, it flashed through her mind that perhaps on this first day of marriage as marriage should be, they might make the first of his sons. And before the pressure of his mouth made thinking impossible, she knew that neither her work on the biography, nor retaining possession of the island, nor being the wife of a man who could adorn her like a queen, had an iota of importance compared with the joy of giving Drogo what *he* wanted.

We are once more on the dangerous edge of burlesque; Drogo ('his ardour revived and ignited the flame in his eyes') is made to sound like a novelty cigarette-lighter, and Annis ('she swayed towards him') like the girl who took one drink too many at the office party. 'Ardour', 'ignited' (a word also coyly used by Ms Cartland), and 'swayed' are of course genteelly lustful euphemisms; one would not expect even a liberated Mills & Boon author to write 'he got another erection' or 'she thrust herself against him', even though peace through intercourse – sanctified intercourse, 'marriage as marriage should be' – is precisely what Ms Weal is talking about. Anne Weal may be a little bolder, more mischievous in implication than Barbara Cartland, but the message is the same gospel of conquest and of the unconditional surrender that is the price of Coming Home. The similes tell the tale. Drogo is 'solid as a rock', Annis is 'soft as a dove'. Her perception of his sexuality, from the 'strong, accelerated heartbeat' to the 'pressure of his mouth' is a perception of the strength and power that mean, for her, security. When he kisses her, thinking becomes impossible. She is content to relinquish all her claims as an independent being, for the 'joy' of giving Drogo what *he* wants. And few readers can be left in any doubt as to what Drogo wants.

'Thinking becomes impossible' is a handy description, literal and ironic, of the usual state of affairs at the end of the paperback romance. Ms Cartland describes her heroine's apperceptive condition in verbs that suggest a progress from sensation to cognition and thence to undifferentiating ecstasy. 'Feel' is overtaken by 'know', and 'know' by heaven knows what:

feel
Lucilla felt a fire rise within her
she felt the world disappear
it was what she had felt when she was with him, etc.
know
ignited, she knew, by the fire in him
ever since she had known him she had changed
now she knew she could never go back

Annis, in Ms Weal's story, also passes through phases of feeling and knowing (though with her, feeling is not so much a perception as an exploratory process):

feel
'you feel as warm and solid as a rock'
'you feel as soft as a dove'
'you can't feel my heart beating'
'no, but I can feel mine'
'she could feel the throbbing of a strong, accelerated heartbeat'
know
she knew that neither her work on the biography, nor . . . etc.

All this feeling and knowing, is of course, the heroine's prerogative. The hero's business is only to take possession of his property.

Still feeling and knowing and doing, they quit the scene, all these shapes and colourful wraiths. They walk away down the steps, they put the helm over, they go back to their wives, they grapple beatifically with their lovers; as the past recedes, as the lessons are learned, as the villains and the fears lie slain, the clock strikes, the sun rises, the long tomorrows put in a first hopeful appearance. Wake, madam. See, they are taking down the screens, and if you lift the window-blind a little you will see a milky luminosity, the shine of early light on clouds, below which, thousands of feet below, stretches our America, our new-found land. And we are all stretching and stirring now, aware of the hot discomfort of feet, the gum and grittiness of eyes, the stale taste of yesterday in the mouth. The flight will be over in an hour or two; and in the meanwhile, here is breakfast and blessed orange juice.

5 Standard ingredients: faces, places, fights, embraces

Quicquid agunt homines, votum timor ira voluptas
Gaudia discursus nostri farrago libelli est.

Whatever people do – praying, fearing, raging,
 pleasuring, rejoicing, gadding about –
That's the hotch-potch of our little book.

(Juvenal, *Satires, I*)

Oh, but don't you hate these things, these landing cards, or whatever they are called? I will never master the craft of filling them in tidily. If they call for block capitals you can be sure that I have already made my play in streaming longhand; my ball-point hawks and spits; the details of my place of birth overrun the allocation of lines and beastly little boxes; and why must they have my passport number when my passport, at the last check, was safely stowed near the bottom of my flight bag, which at the moment is at the very back of the overhead locker, behind Professor Pangloss's greatcoat and his ration of duty-free Glenfiddich? I have to smile though, at the thought of bringing roots, tubers, and illicit foodstuffs into the United States. Our conscience is clear in that respect, madam; not a potato between us, not a daffodil bulb or a can of contraband salmon. Search my case, I can honestly say, you will find no sprig of mint or parsley in my innocent socks, no spinach smuggled in my swimming trunks. I stand before you, an honest man and bona fide traveller. I have nothing to declare.

On reflection, however – the plane yaws and perceptibly drops – I must suppose that we all have something to declare, even though it may not interest the customs and immigration officials. In an hour or so we shall be there, presenting our credentials and our baggage for inspection, patiently showing, on demand, our passport photographs or our underwear, revealing whatever can be decently seen but declaring nothing of our invisible imports, our hungers, prejudices, predilections, predispositions, *votum*, *timor*, *ira*, *voluptas*. I may, after all, have a great deal to declare. I am a psychological contagion and they are going to let me into America for three weeks. If only they knew! Or if only they would take time to ponder my reading matter, because they are all documented there, my sinful fancies: the aggression, the lust, the luxury, the restless envy that motivates so many moral tales. Paperback writers have the devil's own cunning; they allow their readers to emerge with unblemished respectability from vicarious indulgence in emotions and practices routinely denounced from the pulpit or in the better sort of newspaper.

They accommodate our vices by including in their tales some standard ingredients in the form of descriptions or episodes growing out of, but not always wholly essential to, the developing plot. These are often decorative episodes appealing to our Sunday-supplement interest in the hobsnobberies of life among the glamorous and the successful: descriptions of meals, furnishings, dress, jewellery, expensive and powerful cars. There is, however, another kind of standard ingredient, the inclusion of which is often a necessity, or at least a convenient narrative strategy. Descriptions of persons and places occur as routine provisions made by the author for the benefit of the reader seeking to locate the action and visualize the actors. They may be described as having an expository function. Another kind of routine provision, perhaps more appetitive than expository, is the description of fighting – all kinds of conflict, from rude fisticuffs to hi-tech aerial combat – and the portrayal of lovemaking, which on the whole is limited to one kind. That these are standard ingredients is in the nature of the genre. Heroes must all, at some point in the story, have a crack at the foe; heroines must drown in the tides of assenting passion. These are the most popular things in popular fiction.

Figures and faces

It is a general rule of the genre that important characters are described more or less as soon as they enter the story, and that the descriptions are predominantly of face, figure, and dress, rather than of temperament and psychological traits. Romantic fiction observes this principle regularly, even to the extent of allowing a heroine/narrator to describe herself, if there happens to be a mirror handy. It is possibly a little less common in macho fiction, where the male (unless he happens to be a villainous grotesque) is often allowed to enter the action wearing no more descriptive costume than a stock epithet or a decent covering of adjectives:

> Like her, her companion was tall and straight, dark and strong-looking. He guided her to her seat with a brown muscled arm . . .

This is from Wilbur Smith's *Eagle in the Sky*, and follows immediately upon a more protracted and imaginative description of the book's heroine. Or this, from Frederick Forsyth's *The Devil's Alternative*:

> People tended to step aside for him; he was six feet three inches tall, wide as the pavements of the old quarter of the city, blue-eyed and bearded.

The description (of a Norwegian sea-captain – hence the blue eyes and the beard) reflects Mr Forsyth's customary preoccupation with numbers and measurements. Token descriptions of this kind are recurrent in male-orientated narrative, where more elaborately developed verbal portraits are often reserved for heroines, hookers, and *femmes fatales*. The male reader, it is perhaps assumed, will be interested in the actions of men and the physical endowments of women.

King Duncan's assertion that 'there is no art to read the mind's construction in the face' would not be accepted in the world of popular fiction. There is undoubtedly a code, a semiotic system with which all readers are familiar, allocating values to diverse features. Most important are the eyes, which may represent authority in men, if they are 'piercing blue' or 'like chips of blue ice', and tender submission in women if they are 'soft brown'; spiritedness if they are 'sparkling emerald', poetic depth if they are 'misty hazel'. Mouths in women are commonly 'full' and even 'sensuous'; in men, mouths are generally for speaking with, and character is shown by a jawline which is 'firm' and 'clean'. Some women show their breeding with high cheek-bones; others demonstrate their playful charm with noses that may be *retroussé*, but never bent or broken. A man may have a broken nose if it accentuates his rugged good looks, or if he is an attendant character of the cheerful Cockney type; but male noses – fleshy noses, noses with flaring nostrils, cruel acquiline noses,

noses like squabs of formless putty – generally verge on villainy. Hair is a high sign for both sexes: for her, lustrous, opulent, sleek, soft; for him vigorous, thick, groomed; in either case a token and proclamation of sexual vigour and awareness. Mean little women with lifeless locks or slatterns with their hair put up in papers have no place in romance, or are allowed only walk-on parts. Balding men are mildly ridiculous neuters; egg-bald men are full of a sinister and ambiguous promise, which may be of savage impotence or uncontrollable virility. Teeth are sometimes mentioned, as being 'pearly' (hers) or 'white' and 'straight' (his). Some dental irregularity may be allowed to a woman, as a touching, gamine feature, and her ears may be described as small, pink, and delicately whorled. Men's ears are seldom mentioned, except in caricature. On the whole, the ear is a negative attribute, and in any event no description of a face ever begins with the ears. Even the eyebrows and the forehead have precedence.

The face is usually viewed in conjunction with the figure, and here the code is even more obvious and admits of fewer variations. The standard height for a hero is six feet. This is what 'tall' means; under no circumstances could five feet ten and three quarters be construed as 'tall'. The tall man is variously 'slim', 'taut', 'spare', 'muscular', or in some cases 'wiry' (though 'wiry' may suggest someone smaller, and of lower social rank, than the tall man). He is 'perfectly proportioned'. He is often bronzed, and his movements, though casual, are 'lithe', suggesting a controlled tension or the stalking grace of a feral cat. It would be so unconventional as to be a violation of narrative rules for a hero to be a little round pasty-faced fellow with flat feet and a tendency to get stuck in revolving doors, or a mincing wisp of a thing, all wrists and elbows; for these stereotypical degenerates are disqualified from heroship, even though W. H. Auden has rightly reminded us that

> It is the pink and white,
> Fastidious, slightly girling, in the night
> When the proud-arsed broad-shouldered break and run
> Who covers their retreat, dies at his gun.

'Proud-arsed' and 'broad-shouldered' the conventional hero may be, but he must never be *fat*. Large fat men, when they are not comic, are sometimes cast as villains. (The literary tradition goes back to Count Fosco, in Wilkie Collins's *The Woman in White*; and while cinematic examples are many, the classic instance is no doubt that of Sidney Greenstreet.) Heroines, of course, are never fat; they are 'slim', 'slender', and 'graceful'. The standard average height is up to a tall man's chin, which is about five feet four inches. She may be smaller, in which case she is described as *petite*; there is no corresponding category of *grande* for women taller than five feet six inches. The heroine has a 'perfect complexion', her skin being either 'softly pink and white' or sporting a 'glorious golden tan'. Her movements may be quick and decisive or measured and graceful. Her physical properties are either disguised or accentuated by her clothes; very rarely is clothing merely incidental to the way she is presented. The importance of clothes is very clear in this passage from Anne Weal's story, *Summer's Awakening*:

> Among her assets were long-lashed, intelligent grey eyes, a flawless complexion and a beautiful, low-pitched speaking voice. But as she never used make-up and still wore her long thick fair hair in a pigtail dictated by her aunt – although now and then she would rebel and wear it loose about her shoulders – her best features were less noticeable than her worst ones.
>
> From lack of money and other difficulties, she dressed very badly in drab, shapeless, serviceable clothes. Today she was wearing a loose, navy needlecord pinafore over a grey, roll-necked jersey and thick ribbed tights.

The message is clearly encoded: at this point in the story the heroine, Summer, is a little less than glamorous. She will ultimately emerge as a vibrant and passionate beauty, but at the moment she has 'difficulties' – notably a burden of maldistributed flesh resulting from overindulgence in toasted crumpets and butter. In brief, she is fat. It is the description of her wardrobe that carries signals later to be realized as explicit statements. The author could hardly have damned her character more emphatically had she described her as wearing thick red flannel knickers under an old brown gym tunic.

The principal feature of the descriptive technique in this extract is the accumulation of premodified noun phrases – that is, of nouns preceded usually by two or three evaluative adjectives. Thus Summer's physical 'assets' are catalogued:

long-lashed, intelligent grey eyes
flawless complexion
beautiful, low-pitched speaking voice
long thick fair hair

And her items of clothing:

drab, shapeless, serviceable clothes
loose, navy needlecord pinafore
grey, roll-necked jersey
thick ribbed tights

In one instance at least there is a suggestion of a semantic grading of the adjectives, a progression from the general to the particular detail: 'loose' (general character of the garment = 'shapeless'), 'navy' (colour = 'drab'), 'needlecord' (material = 'serviceable'). No regular pattern of grading is observable, however, among the noun phrases in either of the two groups. What does emerge, interestingly, is an implied shift in the value of adjectives occurring both in the 'personal' set and in the 'costume' set. Thus 'grey' and 'thick' have positive connotations in relationship to eyes and hair, but are apparently pejorative in relationship to clothing ('jersey', 'tights') where they suggest drabness and mere serviceability. It is noteworthy that 'serviceable' is here a denigratory term, unfavourably coloured by its association with 'drab', 'shapeless', and 'loose'. Its implied antonym, presumably, is 'glamorous' or 'fashionable'.

Descriptions of clothing are sometimes used in romantic fiction when a familiar character is to be located in a new situation, or when, in accordance with traditional prescription, chrysalis is transformed into butterfly, Cinderella into fairytale princess. In this passage from *Mistral's Daughter*, young Teddy (a woman, like Casey, or Harrie) arrives from her mother's model agency to be photographed by a famous practitioner. She is very nervous:

Her eyelashes were covered in unfamiliar mascara, her skin in powder, base and rouge, artfully applied, and her hair had just been done at Elizabeth Arden. Maggy had turned Teddy out in the flawless adult elegance of Dior's "New Look", choosing a tightly fitted, double-breasted, gray flannel suit with black velvet lapels. The jacket was nipped in savagely at the waist, the hips exaggeratedly rounded by a buckram (sic) lining above a slim skirt that stopped a few inches above her ankles. Teddy wore high-heeled black antelope pumps, a small black velvet hat with a veil that reached below her nose and pale gray kid gloves. Under her expensive new blouse, in spite of the antiperspirant that she had frantically applied three times since the morning, she was beginning to sweat from nerves. She jabbed at the doorbell. Maybe action would keep her dry.

If there is an undertone of the *lasciva puella* in all this – and indeed, she is about to be 'relieved of her baggage of rigid chastity' by the friendly photographer – it may well be because parts of the body are named in contexts that endow the names with something of the guilty vibrancy of dirty words: 'tightly fitted, *double-breasted*'; 'nipped in savagely at the *waist*'; '*hips* exaggeratedly rounded'. The role of adverbs ('tightly, 'savagely', 'exaggeratedly') in these collocations, like that of the verbs ('fitted', 'nipped', 'rounded') seems to be to hint at strenuous acts in a sexual encounter. It is of course no more than a hint, for the willing recipient; nevertheless it does seem that the vocabulary is transiently scented with notions of sexuality.

Again, the noun phrase is the central descriptive structure, but here it is generally more elaborate than in the extract from *Summer's Awakening*. There are several instances of post-modification, when descriptive qualifiers follow the noun headword, and there are examples in which pre- and post-modification combine. These are the constructions that describe Teddy's clothing:

the flawless adult elegance of Dior's "New Look"
a tightly fitted, double-breasted, gray flannel suit with black velvet lapels
the jacket (in anaphoric reference to 'suit', above)
a buckrum lining above a slim skirt that stopped a few inches above her ankles
high-heeled black antelope pumps
a small black velvet hat with a veil that reached below her nose
pale gray kid gloves
her expensive new blouse

The first phrase in the list is the topic phrase, so to speak, the statement of a theme elaborated by subsequent phrases. The same procedure is discernible in the *Summer's Awakening* extract. There, the key words are 'drab', 'shapeless', 'serviceable'; here the theme is represented by 'flawless', 'adult', and 'elegance'. 'Flawless' and 'adult', like 'expensive' and 'new', are evaluative terms implying a dual reference, to the clothes and to their wearer. Colour words acquire a sensuous value in collocation with words naming materials of distinctive texture or sheen: 'gray flannel', 'black velvet', 'black antelope', gray kid'. The passage is, in its linguistic techniques, a kind of extended *double entendre*. The elaborate noun phrases echo the register of the fashion writer or catwalk commentator; but these innocently conventional structures are set in a descriptive procedure that repeatedly brings certain items into an ambiguous or suggestive light.

When an important character is to be introduced for the first time, writers are inclined to say less about costume and more about face and figure. Here is how Catherine Cookson introduces her heroine Tilly Trotter, in the book of that name:

> Tilly Trotter was tall for her age, being now five foot five and a half inches. She was wearing a faded cotton dress and it hung straight from her shoulders to the uppers of her thick boots, and nowhere was there an undulation. Her neck was long and tinted brown with wind and weather, as was her face; yet here there was a flush of pink to the tint on her high cheekbones. Her eyes, now bright and laughing, looked as if they had taken up the colour of her skin, the only difference being that the brown of her skin was matt while the brown of her eyes was clear and deep. Her hair was dark, darker than brown and thick, and it should at her age have been either piled high on top of her head or in a decorous knot at the back, but it was hanging in two long plaits at the back of her neck with what at one time had been a piece of blue ribbon and joined at the ends with a similar piece. Her mouth, full-lipped, was now wide with welcome as she gabbled breathlessly, 'Hello, Simon.'

Catherine Cookson, like Anne Weal, carefully selects those details of appearance and dress that grace and disgrace her heroine. Tilly is graced by the 'flush of pink' on her 'high cheekbones', by her eyes, which are 'bright and laughing', with a brown which is 'clear and deep', and by her hair which is 'dark, darker than brown and thick'. She is disgraced by her clothes: by the 'faded cotton dress' in which there is no 'undulation', by the 'thick boots', and by 'what at one time had been a piece of blue ribbon'. Here, as in the extract from *Summer's Awakening*, the adjective 'thick' does double duty, as a word carrying pejorative connotations (in 'thick boots') and as a word of positive import (in 'her hair was . . . thick'). Otherwise, a key adjective in the rather brief description of her clothing is 'faded'; this is in contrast with the indications of strong and nuanced colour in her facial appearance – the 'flush of pink', the 'matt' brown of the skin, the 'clear and deep' brown of the eyes, the 'darker than brown' of her hair. The one touch of colour in the description of her dress refers to a colour that has faded ('what at one time had been a piece of blue ribbon'). The one allusion to shape is negative, almost comic: there is no 'undulation' in her dress from shoulder to ankle, no hint of swathing or sheathing or figure-hugging, nipping in at the waist or accentuating the line of the hips. Cookson rather obviously chooses to reject the enhancements of the wardrobe, in order, no doubt, to make us read more attentively the character written into the weather-beaten face.

What is quite striking about the sentences describing Tilly's figure and face is that they are right-branching, developing their descriptions in clauses that follow the nouns denoting significant features, rather than making brief adjectival jottings before the noun. Thus, instead of 'She had clear, deep brown eyes', we read:

> Her eyes, now bright and laughing, looked as if they had taken up the colour of her skin, the only difference being that the brown of her skin was matt while the brown of her eyes was clear and deep.

This expository technique allows the writer to elaborate, analyze, qualify, even to make comparisons. What it presents to the reader is not so much a photograph or a dossier as an explanatory discussion; the reader is invited to take part in reasonings and differentiations. Symptoms of this invitation to the reader are 'yet' and 'as if' and 'the only difference being' and 'should have been'. Such notes of cautious qualification run through the passage until, in the final sentence, we meet a statement that makes no reservation, provision, or comparison, and does not seek the reader's assent: 'Her mouth, full-lipped, was now wide with welcome . . .' A descriptive polarity is thus completed. Tilly's dress may be 'faded', but her face is 'full-lipped'. Take this hint, the author tells us; be prepared to discover, under the shabby exterior, a generously passionate nature.

This passage by Catherine Cookson, with its right-branching sentences and frequent expressions of contrast, comparison, or modification, suggests a stylistic distinction that may be illustrated in the following way:

(a) She had extraordinarily deep brown eyes.
(b) Her eyes were of a brown so deep that on occasion it might appear to the casual observer as black.

Sentence (a) presents its material 'pre-scriptively', in a literal sense: the description of the eyes is contained in the adjectives that premodify the noun. In sentence (b), the method is 'post-scriptive'; the relevant noun heads the sentence, as its 'thematic' item, and the description follows, here in an extended complement after the verb 'be'. Writers, introducing their characters, may use both pre-scriptive and post-scriptive techniques:

> Anne's attention had also been drawn to Jennifer North, who was now surrounded by photographers. The girl was undeniably beautiful. She was tall, with a spectacular figure. Her white dress, shimmering with crystal beads, was cut low enough to prove the authenticity of her remarkable cleavage. Her long hair was almost white in its blondeness. But it was her face that held Anne's attention, a face so naturally beautiful that it came as a startling contrast to the theatrical beauty of her hair and figure. It was a perfect face with a fine square jaw, high cheekbones and intelligent brow. The eyes seemed warm and friendly, and the short, straight nose belonged to a beautiful child, as did the even white teeth and the little-girl dimples. It was an innocent face, a face that looked at everything with breathless excitement and trusting enthusiasm, seemingly unaware of the commotion the body was causing. A face that glowed with genuine interest in each person who demanded attention, rewarding each with a warm smile. The body and its accouterments continued to pose and undulate for the staring crowd and flashing cameras, but the face ignored the furor and greeted people with the intimacy of meeting a few new friends at a gathering.

Unlike Catherine Cookson, Jacqueline Susann (this is from her *Valley of the Dolls*) opts for undulations in flesh and fabric alike; Jennifer's 'body and its accouterments' 'pose and undulate for the staring crowd and the flashing cameras'. We are the 'staring crowd' and Anne, here a viewpoint character, is our 'flashing camera'.

The sentences themselves undulate in post-scriptive mimicry of Jennifer's charms:

> Her white dress, shimmering with crystal beads, was cut low enough to prove the authenticity of her remarkable cleavage.

This obscurely tantalizing assertion seems to mean that her dress was cut low enough to show that her breasts were her own. So much for the dress. As for the face:

> But it was her face that held Anne's attention, a face so naturally beautiful that it came as a startling contrast to the theatrical beauty of her hair and figure.

In these two examples, the key words, 'dress' and 'face', precede trains of construction in which subordinate clauses ('to prove the authenticity', etc., 'that it came as a startling contrast', etc.) are linked with antecedents ('enough', 'so') suggesting a process of qualification striving for completeness and accuracy. In each case, however, the appearance of mature consideration, of something said with due regard for descriptive totality, is quite specious. All that the author is telling us is that her subject has the face of an innocent and the body of a courtesan.

This post-scriptive technique incorporates many instances of pre-scriptive shorthand in the form of nouns modified by more or less conventional adjectives:

> It was *a perfect face* with *a fine square jaw, high cheekbones* and *intelligent brow*. The eyes seemed warm and friendly, and *the short, straight nose* belonged to a *beautiful child*, as did *the even white teeth* and *the little-girl dimples*.

Collectively these phrases make up an Identikit picture of a kind so grotesque that it becomes very difficult to visualize; we are asked to supply a 'fine square jaw' and 'high cheekbones', in the fashion-model convention, but to inset a 'short, straight nose' and 'little-girl dimples', in response to the author's evident perception of her character as one who, for all the gross seductiveness of her cleavage, is an innocent child at heart. The adjectival pre-scriptions do not add up to a convincing portrait, but they do correspond to a popular notion, the piquant, subpornographic appeal of the ingenuous spirit in the knowing flesh, the little-girl soul in the big-girl body.

The sentences quoted above, describing Jennifer's face, begin a narrative process in which, almost imperceptibly, the face and the body are presented as agents operating independently of the personality they supposedly represent. Thus, 'it was a perfect face' becomes 'it was an innocent face', and then, with a syntactic shift that makes 'face' the theme of the construction:

a face that looked at everything with breathless excitement, etc.

and:

a face that glowed with genuine interest in each person, etc.

and so to:

the body and its accouterments continued to pose and undulate, etc.

and further:

but the face ignored the furor and greeted people, etc.

At this point it is not simply the case that Jennifer's looks act for Jennifer; face and body have now become independent agents in rivalry with each other.

But is this a perception mediated by Anne, the viewpoint character, or has the author herself, dismissing the convenient bystander, assumed the interpretative role? There seems to be a point in this description – the point, indeed, at which the face-as-object becomes the face-as-agent – when the omniscient author intervenes in order to elaborate observations at first assigned to the onlooker-in-the-story. The face is perhaps an obvious representative of the character; in the following passage, from Wilbur Smith's *The Leopard Hunts in Darkness*, the author boldly focuses on a less obvious choice, the hand:

She had been sitting well back in the gloom at the back of the booth, but now she leaned forward and held out her hand. The spotlamp caught the hand, and so it was the first impression that Craig had of her.

The hand was narrow with artistic fingers, but though the nails were scrubbed clean, they were clipped short and unpainted, the skin was tanned to gold with prominent aristocratic veins showing bluish beneath it. The bones were fine, but there were callouses at the base of those long straight fingers – a hand that was accustomed to hard work.

Craig took the hand and felt the strength of it, the softness of the dry cool skin on the back and the rough places on the palm, and he looked into her face.

She had dark thick eyebrows that stretched in an unbroken curve from the outer corner of one eye to the other. Her eyes, even in the poor light, were green with honey-coloured specks surrounding the pupil. Their gaze was direct and candid.

"Sally-Anne Jay," Ashe said. "This is Craig Mellow."

Her nose was straight but slightly too large, and her mouth too wide to be beautiful. Her thick dark hair was scraped back severely from the broad forehead, her face was as honey-tanned as her hands and there was a fine peppering of freckles across her cheeks.

In this description there are two character-indices: first – an unconventional procedure – the hand, and only in the second instance the face. In both cases the author is careful to speak of his heroine's appearance in terms that imply the tensions and contradictions of an 'interesting' character. She is A *but* B. Her hand tells the tale of a well-bred girl who is a working girl. The fingers are 'artistic', 'long', and 'straight', the veins are 'aristocratic', the bones are 'fine', *but*: the fingernails are 'scrubbed' and 'clipped short', there are 'callouses' at the base of the artistic fingers, and the hand is 'accustomed to hard work'. She is part-nymph, part-navvy, and her hand shows it: the back is 'soft', 'cool', and 'dry' (a sweaty hand disqualifies), but the palm has 'rough places'.

She is also part-belle, part-buddy, as the description of the face tells us. She has nice eyes ('green with honey-coloured specks', even in a poor light), a straight nose, 'thick, dark hair', a broad forehead, and a honey-gold tan; along with a one-piece eyebrow, a large mouth, freckles, and an excessively strict coiffure (not 'combed back', but *scraped*). Her beauty is out of the Middle Ages – the 'narrow' hand, the 'long, straight fingers', the 'fine' bones, the 'broad forehead' might have been pre-scribed by Chaucer or Cranach – but her 'scrubbed', 'clipped', 'scraped', 'stretched', 'freckled' energy are out of the age of safari suits and the liberated lass. It is to Craig that she will eventually surrender herself ('Welcome home, my darling', he says in the penultimate sentence), and so it is appropriate that we should first see her through his eyes, and, indeed, even more appropriate that our first contact with her should be Craig's first touch. It is skilfully done, and the responses of the reader are manipulated with some subtlety. That is more than might be said for this example of a first encounter:

Mr Big sat looking at him, his huge head resting against the back of the tall chair. He said nothing.

Bond at once realized that the photographs had conveyed nothing of this man, nothing of the power and the intellect which seemed to radiate from him, nothing of the over-size features.

It was a great football of a head, twice the normal size and very nearly round. The skin was grey-black, taut and shining like the face of a week-old corpse in the river. It was hairless, except for some grey-brown fluff above the ears. There were no eyebrows and no eyelashes and the eyes were extraordinarily far apart so that one could not focus on them both, but only on one at a time. Their gaze was very steady and penetrating. When they rested on something, they seemed to devour it, to encompass the whole of it. They bulged slightly and the irises were golden round black pupils which were now wide. They were animal eyes, not human, and they seemed to blaze.

The nose was wide without being particularly negroid. The nostrils did not gape at you. The lips were only slightly everted, but thick and dark. They opened only when the man spoke and then they opened wide and drew back from the teeth and the pale pink gums.

There were few wrinkles or creases on the face, but there were two deep clefts above the nose, the clefts of concentration. Above them the forehead bulged slightly before merging with the polished, hairless crown.

Curiously, there was nothing disproportionate about the monstrous head. It was carried on a wide, short neck supported by the shoulders of a giant. Bond knew from the records that he was six and a half foot tall and weighed twenty stone, and that little of it was fat. But the total impression was awe-inspiring, even terrifying, and Bond could imagine that so ghastly a misfit must have been bent since childhood on revenge against fate and against the world that hated because it feared him.

This is in one important respect unlike any of the face-and-figure passages hitherto quoted: it does not play the encoding game of allowing appearances to bespeak the character, but imposes an authorial view to which the description is subordinated. This imposition is emphatically apparent at the beginning of the extract:

> Bond at once realized that the photographs had conveyed nothing of this man, nothing of *the power and the intellect which seemed to radiate from him* . . .

And at the end, in summary:

> But the total impression was awe-inspiring, even terrifying, and *Bond could imagine that so ghastly a misfit must have been bent since childhood on revenge against fate and against the world that hated because it feared him.*

The key words here are 'seemed' and 'could imagine'; they relate the description directly to Bond, not to Bond the observer but to Bond the interpreter acting on behalf of Fleming the author who here introduces his villain and takes the opportunity to slip in a quick psychological note. We cannot fairly deduce that an improbably enormous head betokens powerful intellect combined with a vindictive attitude to society, but Fleming insists on our believing this. If we can believe at all, it is because 'seems' is the verb that licenses belief, or at least permits temporary acceptance of intemperate propositions:

> When they rested on something, they seemed to devour it, to encompass the whole of it.
> . . . . . .
> They were animal eyes, not human, and they seemed to blaze.

If we cancel 'seemed to' and read 'they devoured', 'encompassed', 'they blazed', these assertions are immediately removed from the sphere of the acceptably figurative to the plane of the less acceptably literal.

But there is a tension in the passage between the literal and the figurative, between 'is' and 'seems'. On the one hand, the author's imagination is evidently engaged with the grotesque semblances of a comic-book world:

It was a great football of a head, twice the normal size . . .
. . . . . .

There were no eyebrows and no eyelashes and the eyes were
extraordinarily far apart so that one could not focus on them
both, but only on one at a time.

Considered as literal assertions these are clearly absurd; at a
rough estimate his eyes would have to be at least a foot apart
and his head nearly two feet long from crown to chin. But who
cares? This is not a man, this is the wicked giant in the beanstalk
castle. On the other hand, Fleming does appear to care, at least
to the extent of wanting to give his grotesque fantasy an air of
verisimilitude. His concern appears in the use of a word like
'everted', a textbook term, scientifically dispassionate. More generally, the pretensions of documentary fact are urged in the
frequent clauses constructed on the verb 'be':

It was a great football of a head . . .
The skin was grey-black . . .
It was hairless . . .
There were no eyebrows . . .
the eyes were extraordinarily far apart . . .
Their gaze was very steady and penetrating.
They were animal eyes . . .
The lips were only slightly everted . . .
There were few wrinkles or creases on the face . . .
there was nothing disproportionate about the monstrous
head . . .
It was carried on a wide, short neck . . .

Though the sense of the passage, and the reader's willingness
to accept it in good humour, require always the concession of
'seem' and 'imagine', the claims of 'be', of the required reality
within the fantasy, are urged from sentence to sentence.

A clause that encapsulates Fleming's descriptive intention is
the one reading 'there was nothing disproportionate about the
monstrous head'. This is strictly illogical if the words are taken
at their face value; something monstrous must by definition be
disproportionate. Fleming's concern, however, is not so much
with the logic of his descriptions as with the possibility of eating
his narrative cake and having it. He wants us to accept that the
monster is credibly a man, however monstrous he may seem,
and he repeatedly urges this acceptance upon us through the

use of negatives and other reductive expressions. Here are some (italics added):

> The nose was wide *without* being particularly negroid.
> The nostrils *did not* gape at you.
> The lips were *only slightly* everted.
> They opened *only* when the man spoke . . .
> There were *few* wrinkles . . .
> there was *nothing* disproportionate about the monstrous head.
> Bond knew . . . that *little of it* was fat.

This parade of negatives and downgraders leads us, proposition by proposition, to the culminating assertion: 'But the *total impression* was awe-inspiring.' The 'total impression' is one that the author imposes upon us, instructing us in experiences we are never likely to have. Nowhere in the extract is this more apparent than in the extraordinary description of Mr Big's skin:

> The skin was grey-black, taut and shining like the face of a week-old corpse in the river.

If practical experience were always necessary for the understanding of simile, figurative language would be beyond the general reach. Nevertheless, one is entitled to wonder how many people, including Ian Fleming, might be acquainted with the appearance of a 'week-old corpse in the river'. The figure is merely lurid without being illuminating; a pseudo-simile. It strengthens the conviction mentioned earlier, that Fleming's narrative world is essentially that of the comic book (the old terms, 'penny dreadful' and 'twopenny blood' say it exactly), although his style attempts continual adjustments for the benefit of the adult, 'sophisticated' reader.

Places

In practice, it appears, descriptions of people are considered more important than descriptions of the settings and locations in which the people move; or at any rate it is rather easy to leaf through a paperback and find several extensive accounts of face and figure, whereas descriptions of landscape, townscape, houses, rooms, etc., are briefer and less frequent. They commonly occur at the beginning of a story, when they can be quite long, and subsequently at shifts of narrative location, when they are usually short. In general, they exemplify the convention that the setting is in some way a portent and emblem of action and character. A typical instance is the extract (see p. 89) from Claudia Jameson's *Escape to Love*, describing the study of the masterful Don Carlos; his imposing nature is expressed in the very proportions of the room and the size of the desk at which he sits.

When a particular location is central to a narrative, as a stage set is central to a drama, authors will sometimes provide a factual orientation, with dimensions, compass bearings, relative positions, details of fabric and structure, and general notes, in guidebook fashion, on the history, provenance, and architectural peculiarities of buildings. Fifty years ago Stella Gibbons made fine sport of this convention in her imperishably funny *Cold Comfort Farm*:

> The farm was crouched on a bleak hill-side, whence its fields, fanged with flints, dropped steeply to the village of Howling a mile away. Its stables and out-houses were built in the shape of a rough octangle surrounding the farm-house itself, which was built in the shape of a rough triangle. The left point of the triangle abutted on the farthest point of the octangle, which was formed by the cowsheds, which lay parallel with the big barn. The out-houses were built of rough-cast stone, with thatched roofs, while the farm itself was partly built of local flint, set in cement, and partly of some stone brought at great trouble and enormous expense from Perthshire.
>
> The farm-house was a long, low building, two-storied in parts. Other parts of it were three-storied. Edward the Sixth had originally owned it in the form of a shed in which he housed his swineherds, but he had grown tired of it, and had it rebuilt in Sussex clay. Then he pulled it down. Elizabeth had rebuilt it, with a good many chimneys in one way and another. The Charleses had let it alone; but William and Mary had pulled it down again, and George the First had rebuilt it. George the Second, however, burned it down. George the Third added another wing. George the Fourth pulled it down again.

The front door of the house, this admirable spoof goes on to inform us, faces a ploughed field, so that the occupants are obliged always to enter by the back door; furthermore, there is a corridor that runs half way along the second storey and then stops, so that there is no access to the attics.

Stella Gibbons amuses herself at the expense of the popfiction of her own day ('fanged with flints' is one of her many parodic swipes at the style of the then enormously popular Mary Webb), but the convention she here mocks lives sturdily on. In Simon Raven's *The Survivors*, for instance, much of the action is located in a decaying Venetian *palazzo* tenanted by a devious and peder-astic Greek businessman. (Erotic decadence, class, money, skul-duggery, and a touch of scholarship make up the hotchpotch or cocktail of this author's *oeuvre*.) An orientation is accordingly provided, in a description of the Palazzo Albani's central feature, the dining-room:

It ran the whole length (from the Rio Dolfin to the Calle Alba) of the Palazzo, making a long rectangle which was broken only by a convex curve, formed by a segment of the anteroom, in the central portion of the inner wall. All along this wall were bracketed candelabra, those on the circumference of the curve being of nine branches (in tiers of five, three, and one) and of sumptuous design. The doorway (in the centre of the con-vexity) was surmounted by a pediment which displayed a frieze of the deserted Ariadne . . .

All of this was beguiling enough, but the chief excellence of the room lay not in the room itself, not in the candelabra nor in the friezes, nor even in the magnificent black table that ran on legs carved as gods and heroes for thirty yards down the middle; it lay in the view which was then to be had from any of the seven windows which were set along the outer side wall. Framed between thin stone shafts which supported ogival canopies, they were absolutely plain both in surface and in substance; and what one saw through them was this:

On the right a wall, which rose sheer beside the waters of the Rio Dolfin to a height of twenty feet and was an immediate continuation of the facade of the Palazzo. To the left of this wall, an enclosed garden. In the centre of the garden a gravel path, forming a perfect square and flanked by rose bushes and statuary; within the square an unkempt lawn; at its centre a fountain – a nymph pouring from an urn, looking sadly at the ground as well she might, for her urn was dry and no water ran. Outside and all round the square, a pretty wilderness of shrubs and tall grasses and trees, ilex and lady-birch, apple and cherry: and through the wilderness little tracks (much overgrown) running to little clearings (now hard to define) in

which were garden seats of elegant design and painted metal.
To the left of the garden a wall . . . matching, in height and
texture, the wall which separated the garden from the Rio
Dolfin. At the far end of the garden the tall side, masked by
trees up to forty feet but above that absolutely blank, of the
next building along the Rio.

Stella Gibbons's parody wittily challenges the reader to draw,
or at least to visualize, what she describes. It is of course impossible to do so; the topographical and architectural details so
whimsically amassed defy interpretation. She humorously recalls
for her readers the puzzlement of working through other descriptions, with facts, figures, shapes, and sizes meticulously paraded,
and being able to make nothing of them. Simon Raven's description of the *palazzo* never quite reaches the point of teasing the
reader with the elaborately inconceivable. It can be visualized,
as a plausible account of a workable setting; but it verges all the
while on unintentional parody, a mimetic effect of the kind
known to some literary theorists as 'intertextuality'. There is a
discernible symptom of this in the phrase 'a pretty wilderness of
shrubs and tall grasses', which appears to have been caught
from Jane Austen; Lady Catherine de Bourgh speaks to Elizabeth Bennett of 'a prettyish kind of a little wilderness on one
side of your lawn'.

   Such echoes apart, the most prominent stylistic feature of the
passage is its frank exploitation of the very conventions, in lexicon and syntax, that Stella Gibbons mocks. Particularly at the
beginning of the description there is a good deal of geometrical
talk: 'rectangle', 'convex curve', 'circumference of the curve',
'centre of the convexity', 'segment'; and a little further on, 'a
perfect square'. Cold Comfort Farm, with its 'rough octangle'
and the 'rough triangle' which abuts 'on the farthest point of the
octangle' comes treacherously to mind. Then there is a Forsythian particularity about numbers and measurements: 'nine branches', 'five, three and one', 'thirty yards', 'seven windows', 'a
height of twenty feet'. But the dominant and recurrent syntactic
feature is the prepositional phrase expressing direction, distri-
bution, or spatial relationship: 'along this wall', 'in the centre of
the convexity', 'down the middle', 'between thin stone shafts',
'through them', 'on the right', 'to the left', 'to the left of the
garden', 'in the centre of the garden', 'at the far end of the
garden', 'within the square', 'outside and all round the square',

'through the wilderness', 'above that'. The evident intention is to conduct us on a tour of the property, but the cumulative effect of all this orientation is disorientating, as the author perhaps mischievously suspects. Now and then his recursive, right-branching syntax leads us down the garden path into thickets of nowhere; as when he writes of 'little tracks (much overgrown) running to little clearings (now hard to define) in which were garden seats of elegant design and painted metal'. There is a playful indirection here, a suggestion of a verbal maze not at all inappropriate to the general theme of the book; for the elegantly delapidated Palazzo Albani holds at its centre a secret which has to be discovered by prolonged and circuitous enquiry.

The emblematic house, particularly such a house as waits to receive a governess, a companion, a teacher, or nurse, or any other female outsider in genteelly straitened circumstances, is a favoured motif in romantic fiction. The house often stands for mysteries and histories which challenge and resist the new-comer's intrusions. This theme goes back to the popular fictions of the late eighteenth and early nineteenth centuries, the Gothic novels loved by Jane Austen's contemporaries. Here is Henry Tilney, mocking the convention for the benefit of Catherine Morland, as they travel together to Northanger Abbey:

> We shall not have to explore our way into a hall dimly lighted by the expiring embers of a wood fire – nor be obliged to spread our beds on the floor of a room without windows, doors or furniture. But you must be aware that when a young lady is (by whatever means) introduced into a dwelling of this kind she is always lodged apart from the rest of the family. While they snugly repair to their own end of the house, she is formally conducted by Dorothy the ancient housekeeper up a different staircase, and along many gloomy passages, into an apartment never used since some cousin or kin died in it about twenty years before. Can you stand such a ceremony as this?

Henry Tilney is smiling on Jane Austen's behalf, but the Gothic tale-mongers had evidently started something not easily suppressed by mere laughter. This is what happens when Martha Leigh, heroine of Victoria Holt's *Mistress of Mellyn*, arrives at the great house to take up her appointment as governess. She is received by the housekeeper Mrs Polgrey (we are in Cornwall, the country of Tre-, Pol-, and Pen-):

We were in an enormous hall which in the past must have been used as a banqueting room. The floor was of flagged stone, and the timbered roof was so lofty that I felt it must extend to the top of the house. The beams were beautifully carved and the effect decorative. At one end of the hall was a dais and at the back of this a great open fireplace. On the dais stood a refectory table on which were vessels and plates of pewter.

"It's magnificent," I said involuntarily; and Mrs Polgrey was pleased.

"I superintend all the polishing of the furniture myself," she told me. "You have to watch girls nowadays. Those Tapperty wenches are a pair of flibbertigibbets, I can tell 'ee. You'd need eyes that could see from here to Land's End to see all they'm up to. Beeswax and turpentine, that's the mixture, and nothing like it. All made by myself."

"It certainly does you credit," I complimented her.

I followed her to the end of the hall where there was a door. She opened this and a short flight of some half a dozen steps confronted us. To the left was a door which she indicated and after a moment's hesitation, opened.

"The chapel," she said, and I caught a glimpse of blue slate flagstones, an altar and a few pews. There was a smell of dampness about the place.

She shut the door quickly.

"We don't use it nowadays," she said. "We go to the Mellyn church. It's down in the village, the other side of the cove . . . just beyond Mount Widden."

We went up the stairs and into a room which I saw was a dining room. It was vast and the walls were hung with tapestry. The table was highly polished and there were several cabinets in the room within which I saw beautiful glass and china. The floor was covered with blue carpet and through the enormous windows I saw a walled courtyard.

"This is not *your* part of the house," Mrs Polgrey told me, "but I thought I would take you round the front of the house to my room. It's as well you know the lay of the land, as they say."

I thanked her, understanding that this was a tactful way of telling me that as a governess I would not be expected to mingle with the family.

We passed through the dining room to yet another flight of

stairs and mounting these we came to what seemed like a more intimate sitting room. The walls were covered with exquisite tapestry and the chair backs and seats were beautifully wrought in the same manner. I could see that the furniture was mostly antique and that it all gleamed with beeswax and turpentine and Mrs Polgrey's loving care.

"This is the punch room," she said. "It has always been so called because it is here that the family retires to take punch. We follow the old custom still in this house."

At the end of this room was another flight of stairs; there was no door leading to them, merely a heavy brocade curtain which Mrs Polgrey drew aside, and when we had mounted these stairs we were in a gallery, the walls of which were lined with portraits. I gave each of them a quick glance, wondering if Connan TreMellyn were among them; but I could see no one depicted in modern dress, so I presumed his portrait had not yet taken its place among those of his ancestors.

There were several doors leading from the gallery, but we went quickly along it, to one of those at the far end. As we passed through it I saw that we were in a different wing of the house, the servants quarters I imagined, because the spaciousness was missing.

"This," said Mrs Polgrey, "will be your part of the house."

Not quite Henry Tilney's programme for the quailing newcomer, this nevertheless fulfils the Gothic conditions he hints at: the batty housekeeper, the mysterious chapel on which the door is quickly closed (a circumstance which would have aroused Catherine Morland's most thrilling suspicions), the exile of our heroine, up and down stairs, to a remote part of the mansion. Stairs and doors figure here, as indeed they do in *Northanger Abbey*. (Jane Austen writes:'Returning through the large and lofty hall, they ascended a broad staircase of shining oak, which, after many flights and many landing-places, brought them upon a long wide gallery. On one side it had a range of doors . . .') There are 'several doors' leading from the gallery in Mellyn, and there are four flights of stairs between the hall and the servants' quarters. These devices of stage-setting, suggesting mysteries, perplexities, the separations of position and sympathy which the heroine must bridge, characterize a passage the language of which is otherwise conventional to the point of tameness. Adjectives are put about like nondescript little ornaments. The hall is 'enormous', the dining room windows likewise are 'enormous', the dining room itself is 'vast', the roof of the hall is 'lofty'; beams are 'beautifully carved', with a 'decorative' effect, and the general impression that the hall gives is 'magnificent'; the glass and china are 'beautiful', the tapestry is 'exquisite', and the table is 'highly polished'. If it were not for the stairs, the doors, and the spooky chapel, Mellyn might seem as unGothically boring as any other fourth-rate stately home.

Fights

Whether his location is a bar, a barracks, or a boardroom, man's business involves him sooner or later in a fight. These are expected in actionbooks as fencing bouts were expected by the audience in the Elizabethan theatre; and are no doubt as critically relished by the knowing observer. The character called Moose Malloy in Raymond Chandler's *Farewell, My Lovely* ('a big man but not more than five feet six inches tall and not wider than a beer truck') comes into the story fighting, with a minor bout on page two and a major engagement on page twelve, as he reduces the pretensions of an impertinent bouncer:

> The bouncer frowned. He was not used to being talked to like that. He took his hand off the shirt and doubled it into a fist about the size and colour of a large eggplant. He had his job, his reputation for toughness, his public esteem to consider. He considered them for a second and made a mistake. He swung the fist very hard and short with a sudden outward jerk of the elbow and hit the big man on the side of the jaw. A soft sigh went around the room.
>
> It was a good punch. The shoulder dropped and the body swung behind it. There was a lot of weight in that punch and the man who landed it had had plenty of practice. The big man didn't move his head more than an inch. He didn't try to block the punch. He took it, shook himself lightly, made a quiet sound in his throat and took hold of the bouncer by the throat.
>
> The bouncer tried to knee him in the groin. The big man turned him in the air and slid his gaudy shoes apart on the scaly linoleum that covered the floor. He bent the bouncer backwards and shifted his right hand to the bouncer's belt. the belt broke like a piece of butcher's string. The big man

put his enormous hand flat against the bouncer's spine and heaved. He threw him clear across the room, spinning and staggering and flailing with his arms. Three men jumped out of the way. The bouncer went over the table and smacked into the baseboard with a crash that must have been heard in Denver. His legs twitched. Then he lay still.

"Some guys," the big man said, "has got wrong ideas about when to get tough."

For this demonstration of physical superiority backed by simple indifference to the well-being of others, there is a good narrative reason. Ebullient destructiveness is one aspect of Moose Malloy's character. The incongruous collateral aspect is an almost childishly sentimental devotion to a woman called Velma. (It is a dangerous infatuation; she eventually shoots him.) Malloy is a type created by Chandler and taken up by directors of inferior gangster movies: the gorilla with a tender spot for a little lady. There is humour in this paradox, and humour of a wry, laconic sort is a feature of Chandler's style even when he is describing a fight. There is an impish elegance, a touch of oxymoron: 'He had his job, his reputation for toughness, his public esteem to consider. He considered them for a second and made a mistake.' There is humour in the very precision of some statements: not 'People scattered in all directions', but 'Three men jumped out of the way'. Astonishingly violent things are happening, but the stylistic effect throughout is cool, distanced, whimsical. The macho lexicon is represented ('spinning', 'staggering', 'flailing', 'smack', 'crash') without being obtrusive. More striking are the comparisons, 'a fist about the size and colour of a large eggplant', 'the belt broke like a piece of butcher's string', that seem grotesque and at the same time accurate, like the language of a journalist reporting a fight. The feeling of reportage is strengthened by the writer's display of some knowledge of pugilistic technique: 'The shoulder dropped and the body swung behind it.' Such details appeal to the reader as onlooker, rather than as imaginary participant. This effect is most clearly served by the methodical descriptive technique in which sentence after sentence is headed by the subject phrase representing the agent-role: 'The big man turned him . . .', 'He bent the bouncer backwards . . .', 'The big man put his enormous hand flat against the bouncer's spine . . .', 'He threw him clear across the room . . .' No sentence begins with an adverbial, a marked theme, a non-finite clause – 'Clear across the room he threw him . . .', 'Into the baseboard he smacked . . .', 'Turning him in the air, the big man slid his gaudy shoes apart . . .' There is no obvious attempt to raise the excitement by manipulating the syntax. On the contrary, everything is measured, deliberate, exactly observed but almost dispassionate. And this is appropriate, for the observer of this scene is the book's narrator and central figure, the private detective Philip Marlowe, and it is Marlowe's character, as much as if not more than that of Moose Malloy, that is conveyed to us through this narrative: cynically humorous, detached, streetwise, missing nothing. The description of a fight so early in the book is therefore something more than a sop to the famished aggression of the reader on the Clapham omnibus; it has a function that embraces the story and its characters.

Philip Marlowe is a character capable of subtlety; he is often reflective, has moments of sadness and compassion, is, in his way, a moralist. James Bond, on the other hand, is not much better than a licensed delinquent, and his fights, dutifully recorded in every book, have a simple appeal to the latent delinquency of the reader. In this passage from *Live and Let Die* we see him dealing with an uncouth person called The Robber, a minion of the football-headed, wide-eyed Mr Big:

> In the fraction of a second that The Robber's eyes flickered down, Bond's right foot in its steel-capped shoe lashed out to its full length. It kicked the rifle almost out of the Robber's hands. At the same moment that The Robber pulled the trigger and the bullet crashed harmlessly through the glass ceiling, Bond launched himself in a dive at the man's stomach, his two arms flailing.
>
> Both hands connected with something soft and brought a grunt of agony. Pain shot through Bond's left hand and he winced as the rifle crashed down across his back. He bore on into the man, blind to pain, hitting with both hands, his head down between hunched shoulders, forcing the man back and off his balance. As he felt the balance yield he straightened himself slightly and lashed out again with his steel-capped foot. It connected with The Robber's kneecap. There was a scream of agony and the rifle clattered to the ground as The Robber tried to save himself. He was half way to the floor when Bond's uppercut hit him and projected the body another few feet.

The Robber fell in the centre of the passage just opposite what Bond could now see was a drawn bolt in the floor.

As the body hit the ground a section of the floor turned swiftly on a central pivot and the body almost disappeared down the black opening of a wide trap-door in the concrete.

As he felt the floor give under his weight The Robber gave a shrill scream of terror and his hands scrabbled for a hold. They caught the edge of the floor and clutched it just as his whole body slid into space and the six-foot panel of reinforced concrete revolved smoothly until it rested upright on its pivot, a black rectangle yawning on either side.

Well may The Robber vociferate; beneath that trap door there are sharks, to whose maxillary attentions Bond, in a fit of virtuous indignation, will presently consign him. The fight is a typical episode of Bondage. Philip Marlowe's fights necessarily keep some connection with the mean realities of brawling, but Bond in action is all gimmickry and kitsch. There is always the steel-brimmed bowler hat, the bladed boot, the cheese-wire in the handle of the exploding briefcase, the lethal matchbox, or at the very least, as here, an Edward IV Rose Noble with which to distract your opponent before you have at him with your steel-capped evening pumps. Marlowe's reality and Bond's fantasy can even be deduced from the techniques of fighting. Raymond Chandler knows precisely what happens when a fist-fighter throws a punch:

It was a good punch. The shoulder dropped and the body swung behind it.

But Ian Fleming has not really considered what happens when a man 'dives' at his antagonist:

Bond launched himself in a dive at the man's stomach, his two arms flailing.

This sacrifices sense to sensation. You cannot 'dive at' something with your 'two arms flailing'; the flailing disturbs the balance and diverts the aim. The bouncer's arms 'flail' in the Chandler passage; but he is thoroughly off-balance. 'Flailing' in Chandler is descriptively adequate; in Fleming its descriptive pretensions are really subordinate to its sensational appeal as an element in the macho lexicon. This is in general more prominent than in the Chandler extract, or perhaps not so carefully offset by other stylistic elements: 'lashed out', 'kicked', 'crashed', 'launched himself', 'flailing', 'grunt of agony', 'shot through', 'crashed down', 'hitting', 'forcing', 'scream of agony', 'clattered', 'projected', 'scream of terror', 'scrabbled', 'clutched'. There is a further, perhaps more important, contrast between the two passages in the syntax and the underlying narrative procedure. Marlowe's report of the fight between Moose Malloy and the bouncer is characterized, as we have noted, by subject-and-agent headed sentences, with no attempt to link narrative events through introductory adverbials, non-finite clauses, etc. Here in the Fleming passage there are several instances of sentences headed by adverbial constructions:

> In the fraction of a second that The Robber's eyes flickered down, Bond's right foot . . . lashed out to its full length.
> (Query: How long is Bond's right foot, and how far would it extend in a fraction of a second?)

> At the same moment that The Robber pulled the trigger . . . Bond launched himself, etc.

> As he felt the balance yield he straightened himself slightly and lashed out again with his steel-capped foot.

> As the body hit the ground a section of the floor turned swiftly on a central pivot . . . etc.

> As he felt the floor give under his weight The Robber gave a shrill scream of terror . . . etc.

What these constructions project is the notion of simultaneous actions; we may compare this with the strict sequencing, one event at a time, of Marlowe's fight-report. Adverbial clauses, mainly of the 'as' type, also occur within sentences, along with participle and adjectival clauses; all these clause-types carry the sense of simultaneity mentioned above: 'as the rifle crashed down across his back', 'as The Robber tried to save himself', 'just as his whole body slid into space', 'when Bond's uppercut hit him', 'until it rested upright on its pivot', 'his two arms flailing', 'hitting with both hands', 'forcing the man back and off his balance', 'a black rectangle yawning on either side', 'blind to pain', 'his head down between hunched shoulders'. In fact the general syntactic texture of the Fleming passage is very different from that of the Chandler extract, in which there is only one instance of participial elaboration. ('He threw him clear across

the room, spinning and staggering and flailing with his arms'.)
The difference is well encapsulated by these two instances:

Chandler: He took it, shook himself lightly, made a quiet
                sound in his throat and took hold of the bouncer
                by the throat.

Fleming: At the same moment that The Robber pulled the
                trigger and the bullet crashed harmlessly through
                the glass ceiling, Bond launched himself in a
                dive at the man's stomach, his arms flailing.

One does not have to analyse and compare the syntactic structures of these two sentences in order to perceive the stylistic
intention in each case: Chandler's, to take the narrative piece
by particular piece, Fleming's, to take in bundles of hectic
impression. Which is the better fight-piece is for readers to
decide; but it has to be said in Chandler's favour that he is a
more serious craftsman than Fleming. He evidently works on
the principle that a fight in the story should be there for the
story's sake, not for its own; but we cannot always say that the
principle is readily observed by Ian Fleming or by other writers
of actionbooks.

Fist-fighting – the bar brawl, the tussle on the edge of the
snakepit, the punch-up in the warehouse while the clock counts
out the seconds to detonation – is readily translated, given the
necessary technical knowledge on the author's part, into
machine-fighting, which means the car chase, the crude encounter with chain-saws and flame-throwers, the novelty bout with
earth removers and motor cycles, the contest of speedboats, or,
most commonly, the aerial dogfight. In Wilbur Smith's *Eagle in
the Sky* there is a pages-long description of a combat between
an Israeli Mirage fighter, piloted by the hero, David, and a Syrian
MIG piloted by a Russian. This is part of it:

He rolled half out of the turn and then with conscious thought,
reversed the roll. The Mirage shuddered with protest and his
speed bled off. The Russian saw it and came down on him
from high on his starboard quarter. As David pushed the stick
fully forward and left he kicked on full left rudder, ducking
under the blast of cannon fire, and the Mirage went down in
a spiralling dive. The blood which gravity had sucked from
his head was now flung upwards through his body, filling his
head and his vision with bright redness, the red-out of inverted

gravitational force. A vein in his nose popped under the pressure and suddenly his oxygen mask was filled with a flood of
warm choking blood.

The Russian was after him, following him into the dive,
lining him up for his second burst.

David screamed with the metallic salty taste of blood in his
mouth and hauled back on the stick with all his strength, the
nose came up and over, climbing out of the dive, and again
the blood drained from his head – going from red-out to
black-out in the fraction of a second and he saw the Russian
following him up, drawn by the ploy. At the top David kicked
it out in a breakaway roll. It caught the Russian, he was one-
hundredth of a second slow in countering and he swung
giddily through David's gunsight, an almost impossible deflection shot that sluiced cannon fire wildly across the sky, spraying it like water from a garden hose.

Here the macho lexicon projects a power both human and
technological: 'screamed' is strident, but no more evocative of
the straining sinew than 'inverted gravitational force'. Discernible
behind the vocabulary are figurative procedures, perhaps not
wholly realized by the author himself, which make of this dogfight an affair somewhat more complicated than a simple and
strenuous shoot-out between David and the Russian. Their
machines, the Mirage and the MIG, are in correlated conflict
(though this may not emerge so clearly from the present extract);
more than that, David's body is at odds with David. Man fights
man; machine fights machine; man fights machine; blood fights
brain. It is indeed a complex fight, and the complicating factor
is technology, in this case the technology of flying.

Something of this complexity can be brought out by examining
the verbs denoting actions, processes, or events, and considering
the agents – in the wide sense of 'doers' or 'sufferers' – associated with them. These agents turn out to be of at least three
kinds, in recurrent contrast with each other. There is a contrast
of Machine and Man; see how they suffer alike:

Machine: The Mirage *shuddered* with protest . . .
Man: David *screamed* with the metallic salty taste of
             blood, etc.

There is a further contrast of non-animate ('gravity', 'deflection
shot'), and animate; and most striking of all, there is a regular

alternation of holonymic and meronymic, that is, of terms denoting the whole person ('David', 'he') and terms indicating some feature associated with that whole ('blood', 'vein'). In the text, a general balance is struck between the holonymic and non-animate/meronymic agencies, though in reading the passage we may be less immediately aware of this than of the *verbs*, which are forcefully expressive of action or event. Some instances:

Holonymic:

[David]	pushed
[he]	kicked
[he]	ducking
[the Russian]	swung
[David]	hauled

Non-Animate/Meronymic:

[gravity]	sucked
[blood]	was flung
[vein]	popped
[blood]	drained
[deflection shot]	sluiced
[deflection shot]	spraying

The verbs in the 'holonymic' set, both transitive and intransitive, all denote activity of an abrupt and energetic kind. Those in the 'non-animate/meronymic' set also have a component describable as 'energy', 'sudden force'. Beyond that, however, they have, in the case of 'sucked', 'drained', 'sluiced', and 'spraying', a rather interesting connotation: they are all associated with the notion of something *fluid*. In the first instance, the 'fluid' is human blood; but the machine also produces a fluid, in the form of its cannon-shells. The notion of fluidity, and the association of man and machine, is implicit in the incidental imagery of the passage. David's oxygen mask is filled with 'a *flood* of warm choking blood', which gives his mouth 'a *metallic*, salty taste'. The wounded flesh discharges a fluid; the human fluid has the machine-savour of metal.

These instances point to ambivalences, or multivalences, in the text, which are further complicated by the vocabulary of the technical register. A 'second burst' (of cannon fire) is at one level an ordinary descriptive phrase; 'burst' is the word one would use as a matter of course. But a little earlier we have had 'blast of cannon fire', and 'blast' and 'burst' conjointly assume values beyond the factually descriptive. They become, in fact, elements in the macho vocabulary. This ambivalence also affects phrases which ostensibly describe nothing more than the manoeuvres of the aircraft: 'rolled half out of the turn', 'a breakaway roll'. It is the plane which 'rolls', but the reader can hardly avoid associating the word with human actions such as pushing, kicking, and hauling. Phrases such as 'full left rudder' and 'inverted gravitational force' may acquire peculiar energies almost accidentally or contingently, thanks to a reader's tendency to focus discretely on 'full' or 'inverted'. (Both suggest polarities, all-or-nothing extremes.) Certainly the technological vocabulary is not emotionally neutral; the machine acts and suffers with the man.

Embraces

There is in such descriptions a degree of sensuality that can convey the odd impression that the pilot-antagonists – rolling, pushing, swinging giddily – are engaged in a form of love-making; and indeed many descriptions of the romantic embrace might lend themselves to a lexical analysis of doers and doings comparable to the one sketched out above. This depends, it must be said, on the length and intensity of the proceedings; for the scope of the romantic embrace includes the tender, story-concluding kiss, various degrees of genteel groping, and strenuous episodes of particularized intercourse. Best-sellers and block-busters seem to require periodic intercalations of lust, performed with the dutiful solemnity of a work-out in the gym or a visit to the bank. These exercises are as a rule legitimized by the plea of true love, just as James Bond's acts of enthusiastic sadism are legitimized by the plea of patriotic duty. But often enough love has very little to do with it. In Joseph Heller's novel *Good as Gold*, the hero, Bruce Gold, brutally corrects one of his mistresses who ventures to speak of them as 'lovers'. 'We're not lovers', he tells her, 'we're fuckers'. This fine distinction is relevant to many of the carnal exchanges described in romantic fiction; even in novels published by Mills & Boon. The blurb writer may urge the attractions of 'an action packed yarn' or 'a story of torrid passions'; what it amounts to, alas, is the old unquenchable vernacular thirst for slugging and swiving. Men like to describe fights, perhaps because fights are a kind of intercourse. Women have a peculiar gift for talking about the other, perhaps because with them it is a kind of fighting.

The nice girl, fighting off her ardent lover, wages an even fiercer fight against her own treacherous impulses. Here are Suzie and Don Carlos, whose first meeting we have already witnessed, buckling down (if that is the right word) to the business that makes the world go round:

> Suzie closed her eyes, knowing that she should make the effort to go upstairs and go to bed, but reluctant to move. When she heard Carlos' deep voice speak to her it was obvious he was standing very near to her. Her eyes flickered open to see him leaning over her, his face close to hers, far too close for comfort . . .
>
> "You look so desirable, Suzie, sitting there like that, all relaxed and – " And then his mouth was on hers, taking her by surprise and stopping her breath. His arms locked around her, pulling her close against the hardness of his body as he sat down next to her. Like a knife, a sudden panic cut through Suzie's body as her brain screamed out the message that this was wrong – wrong! She struggled futilely against him, trying desperately to push him away, knowing full well that if she succumbed to the ecstasy of his kiss she would be lost, and knowing also that she was fighting against herself. Even as her common sense told her this was pointless and wrong, her lips parted under his as if by a will of their own.
>
> The battle within her ceased, the responsibility for her actions slipping away as her body took command, submitting helplessly to every burning, thrilling touch of Carlos' fingers, taking what it wanted, needed from him. As his lips became more demanding her traitorous body responded to his passion with shocking abandon. His lips moved down from her face to her throat and shoulders, covering her with taunting, tantalising kisses which made her want more and more. Her nipples responded eagerly under his touch and her arms went slowly around his neck, pulling him closer and closer.

And then – oh heavens! – her engagement ring catches in his sweater, recalling her obligations to an absent fiancé, and she disentangles herself, leaving Carlos blanched beneath his suntan, 'his breath coming in rasps'. Suzie's is a very nice morality; she sees no harm in blatantly lying and passing off a deception on a complete stranger, but to be kissed by a man to whom she is not contracted is wrong – wrong! For this she is willing to put up a fight; and indeed it is remarkable how much, in this respect, the vocabulary of erotic encounters seems to draw on the same sources as the machoman's lexicon. The sensations of Suzie on the sofa are not so far, lexically, from those of David in the sky. David '*screamed* with the metallic salty taste of blood in his mouth'; Suzie's brain '*screamed* that this was wrong'. She is engaged in desperate conflict – 'struggled', 'fighting', 'battle' are words that tell us this – and it is a conflict expressed, inasmuch as physical action is involved, in verbs such as 'locked', 'pulling', 'push'. Where the description moves into a somewhat different range of vocabulary is in the evocation, mainly through adjectives, of erotic sensations and responses: 'burning', 'thrilling', 'taunting', 'tantalising'. Suzie's fight lapses into helpless abandonment, a helplessness which is projected through the recurrence, throughout the extract, of non-animate or meronymic agents:

> Her eyes flickered open . . .
> his mouth was on hers . . .
> Like a knife, a sudden panic cut through Suzie's body . . .
> her brain screamed out the message that this was wrong . . .
> Even as her common sense told her . . .
> her lips parted under his as if by a will of their own
> her body took command, submitting helplessly, etc.
> As his lips became more demanding . . .
> her traitorous body responded to his passion . . .
> His lips moved down from her face to her throat, etc.
> Her nipples responded eagerly under his touch . . .
> her arms went slowly around his neck, etc.

There are in fact no more than eight finite clauses in the quoted passage that have 'Suzie' or 'she' in the subject position, representing the agent role. Such constructions, together with their non-finite dependents, represent Suzie battling for command, as in the following sample:

> She struggled futilely against him, trying desperately to push him away, knowing full well that if she succumbed to the ecstasy of his kiss she would be lost, and knowing also that she was fighting against herself.

But at the beginning of the paragraph that ensues the above quotation, the syntactic/semantic procedure emphatically changes, signalling that the battle is over:

The battle within her ceased, the responsibility for her actions slipping away as her body took command, submitting help-lessly to every burning, thrilling touch of Carlos' fingers, taking what it wanted, needed from him.

Those two sentences might be taken conjointly as paradigmatic of the change from struggle to surrender which characterizes many a romantic embrace.

The theme of love-making as combat recurs in some descrip-tive essays couched in a bolder, more explicit style than Claudia Jameson's relatively modest account of how Suzie almost surren-dered herself. In Judith Krantz's *Mistral's Daughter*, Maggy Lunel, a virgin, succumbs to the great man. The episode is a version of the erotic archetype, the painter and his model; later in the book, Maggie's daughter Teddy similarly enacts the fable of the model and the photographer. It is a peculiarity of the genre that spirited girls never give themselves to dentists or tree-surgeons; artists and such win the favours every time. But here is the artist Mistral, about to consummate his desires after a page and a half of preparatory hanky-panky:

Still kneeling, sitting on his heels, holding her waist in both hands, Mistral launched himself into her body. She was so moist that he was able to advance several inches before he reached the barrier. He persisted, not understanding, and got no farther.

"What . . .?" he murmured, heat consuming him as he looked down at the darkness of the triangle where they were joined. He tried again, without success. Now, the spell of inaction broken, Maggy gathered herself up with all her cour-age and pressed forward, willing herself to open to him. Every muscle in her long, strong legs was tensed, her toes were pointed, her hands clutched the mattress, and her back arched as she raised her pelvis upward, his jutting, hot spur of flesh the only focus in the universe. There was a flash of pain but she ignored it, launching herself anew, met halfway by his mighty thrust. Suddenly he was inside of her, suddenly the spear, point and shaft and hilt, now a heavy fullness of mortal flesh, was encompassed by her body and they lay still, panting like gladiators evenly matched who pause to salute each other before renewing the struggle.

At the end of this we readers are entitled to say that we get the idea; but that it sounds very uncomfortable. The piece is written in terms of attack and counter-attack: 'Mistral launched himself into her body'; 'Maggy gathered herself up with all her courage and pressed forward'. The author politely avoids the word 'penis', but resorts with evident relish to synonyms of weaponry – 'his jutting, hot spur of flesh', 'the spear, point and shaft'. The lovers are 'gladiators evenly matched', one throwing off her 'spell of inaction' to meet the other's 'mighty thrust'. It is a conceit that must have been old when King Alfred was a stripling. To write about coupling with an originality that goes beyond the standard tour of the erotic state – the nipples, always 'pointed', the breasts, 'perfectly formed', the thighs ('straining'), the 'dark triangle', the flesh in general ('exquisitely silken') – calls for resources that the inflated currency of popfiction is always threatening to bankrupt. Publishers encourage it, because they suppose that readers hunger for it; and writers, in a baffled, sweating style, do their best to provide it. Their bafflement lurks in some grammatical stereotypes. It might be thought, for example, that any description of His and Hers in the great bedroom boxing exhibition would be high on transitivity: 'He kissed her passionately', 'She seized him', etc. But the incidence of transitive constructions (verb + direct object) is as a rule much lower than the occurrence of intransitive verbs or verbs complemented by a reflexive pronoun. She 'feels helpless'; she 'feels herself melting away'; only here and there does she 'feel' *him* or *his*. In the gladiatorial encounter of Mistral and Maggy, transitive constructions are relatively few; there are, in fact, eight, five of which turn up in non-finite and subordinate clauses ('holding her waist in both hands', 'heat consuming him', 'before renewing the struggle', 'before he reached the barrier', 'who pause to salute each other'). The verb in main clauses is most frequently 'be'; but there is a large number of clauses with intransitive or reflexive verbs (e.g. 'he persisted', 'he tried again', 'they lay still', 'Mistral launched himself', 'Maggy gathered herself up', 'willing herself to open to him'). These reflexive engagements and intransitive transactions, together with the meronymic agents that turn up on cue ('every muscle . . . was tensed', 'her toes were pointed', 'her hands clutched the mattress', 'her back arched') collectively make the strange impression that each of the lovers is preoccupied with a very strenuous, achingly self-absorbed activity, for which the other's attendant presence is required.

It is more athletic than erotic; *c'est magnifique, mais ce n'est*

pas l'amour. It is not like that tender and terrific moment towards
the end of *Emma* when Miss Woodhouse confesses that once,
in a moment of unguarded amiability, she called Mr Knightley
'George'. Now *there* is a revelation, an indiscretion, a passion,
there is a yearning and a wonder of loving beyond all your red
mists and silken thighs that strain to the touch of hungry fingers,
etcetera, that stray irresistibly down to where, etcetera, seeming
to devour, etcetera. I think so, madam, I really do. George, you
will note – not Dominic or Carlos or Gregory. You will not find
Mr Knightley's symmetrically sculpted supertan on the cover of
a Mills & Boon. You will not see *his* eyes glinting with lazy
mockery as he deftly dismantles a corsage. And yet is not Mr
Knightley a considerable lover? George – the very name brings
us coolly down to earth – whither we now tend – for the flight
is nearly over – bells ring, lights flash, our captain commandingly
squawks – I fasten my seat-belt, you fasten your seat-belt, he
fastens his seat-belt – the smokers all stop smoking – I am going
deaf – my popping ear-drums admit a horrid roar of engines –
I am going deaf again – I shut my eyes and think of Mr Knightley,
that sane, reasonable, unromantic, horse-age man – there is a
lurching, a rushing upwards incredibly and unrolling swift of
runway – and we touch, with a buffet and a squeak, and we
romp along the receiving shore, and oh, we are down. The
Americans all break into applause, as though a conductor had
turned on the podium or a leading actor had come out to take
his curtain call. Bravo, indeed, bravo. As for me, I cannot judge
the quality of the performance; but we have made the flight,
and it is good to have arrived, and I am happy now to quit the
plane, making sure that I have all my belongings with me.

Postscript: and so to bed

When that I was and a little tiny boy,
  With hey, ho, the wind and the rain,
A foolish thing was but a toy.
  For the rain it raineth every day.
                    (Shakespeare, *Twelfth Night*)

HE:
Exactly one hour and twenty-seven minutes after the Boeing
747 of British Airways flight SE262 touched down in a perfect
landing at Seatac International Airport, Jonathan Doe, better
known in certain dingy offices as Ivan Dubkovic, stood in line
with a little group of weary travellers waiting for the limousine
to come and take them to the Mogadon Hotel. Tired though he
was after eight hours and forty-three minutes in the air at a
cruising height of 28,000 feet, Jonathan Doe's keenly observant
eyes moved restlessly behind his steel-rimmed Dollond and Ait-
chison bifocals, watching, precisely recording every event, allowing no detail to escape his vigilance. To miss anything at this
point, he realized, would be to imperil the mission he was about
to complete, the complex operation that had begun one morning
precisely four months earlier when he had walked through a
door marked Simcox and Flute, Travel Agents. Remembering
that day, he laughed mirthlessly, with an almost imperceptible
shaking of the broad shoulders in the perfectly-cut Harris Tweed
jacket. Sensing a movement behind him, he whirled around,
teeth clenched, to confront . . .
SHE:
. . . his glamorous companion, Charley Doe, whose ethereal
features, softly framed in glowing brown hair coiffured with
exquisite casualness, could be recognized on the covers of a
dozen-and-one fashion magazines as those of Kathryne de
Launay, the internationally-famous model who had emerged
from nowhere to take the world of fashion and glamour by

storm. Only Jonathan, her husband, to whom she was secretly
married, knew the whole truth: that Kathryne de Launay's per-
iodical absences from the fashion scene always coincided with
the beginning of term at the comprehensive school where Charley Doe taught English, Book-keeping, and some Netball. They
had not told their neighbours anything of her fashion career, still
less of Jonathan's dangerous work as a free-lance espionage
agent. It had been easier to keep themselves to themselves,
living quietly on Jonathan's salary as a famous University Lecturer, saving up by dribs and drabs for this holiday. Charley stole
a tender glance at her husband's handsome face, glorying in the
confident authority of its firm jawline, loving the wisp of hair
that kept falling boyishly into his china-blue eyes. Here, she
thought . . .

HE:

. . . it comes, said Jonathan Doe, and his stomach tightened
convulsively as the hotel limo, a two-tone Dodge truck with a
brown vinyl roof, lurched into the parking bay with a scream of
brakes, jerking to a halt not three feet six inches away from
where Doe crouched over his brown Samsonite valise, ready to
spring into action as soon as the doors opened. For a moment
he had a glimpse of the driver's face, a mask of savagery, the
mouth a grinning gash below a swarthily sensual nose and two
eyes that had the evil gloss of pebbles in wet sand. Quickly he
sized up the situation. The driver was coming towards him fast.
Not far away was the Frenchman. He could not see Charley,
but he heard her sharp intake of breath when the driver said . . .

SHE:

. . . 'You folks all for the Mogadon?'

Somehow the American accent sounded so strange, so
different from anything she had known before. Leading a sophisticated and varied life as she did, she knew, of course, that
American English and her own flawless British accent would be
different in many respects, but the driver's confident command
of the foreign idiom had a vibrancy that took her utterly by
surprise. It made her tremulously aware of him as a man, a man
looking at her, his dark, hungry eyes devouring her body, feast-
ing on the curvature of her outrageously expensive blouse and
figure-hugging skirt. All her powers of resistance draining away,
she could only falter 'Yes, we're for the Mogadon,' and stumble
forward, in her confusion completely forgetting her handbag.

'Madame?' That rather sweet old French gentleman who sat

next to her on the plane proferred her imitation alligator *sac à main* with a gesture of exquisite courtliness. 'C'est à vous?'

'Oui.' Charley gasped, realizing too late that in an unguarded second she had answered him in fluent idiomatic French. Self-reproach clawed at her, but his eyes on hers were reassuring.

'Have no fear,' he said, quietly, his perfect English touched by the merest trace of a Parisian burr. 'Your secret is safe with me.'

Charley longed to ask this mysterious stranger how he had divined the truth that had eluded so many others for so long, but Jonathan was speaking to her, urgently, curtly, hurtfully.

'Come on, Charley.'

Shocked beyond measure and blinking back the hot tears that made a scalding mess of her mascara, she fled into the waiting limo. How could he . . .

HE:

. . . be so predictable? Ivan Dubkovic, his brains whirling, scented a trap. This could so easily be a set-up, if the driver and Frenchy were in league, and it was beginning to look that way. One glance at the outsize pocket of the Frenchman's distinctly grimy trench-coat had been enough to convince him that it contained a Walther LP 53 recoilless pneumatic-action pistol. Lethal at short range, requiring no silencer and making no fumes, it was a weapon ideally adapted to the elimination of an opponent if you could lure him into a hotel limousine. Dubkovic smiled inwardly, appreciating the skill of the manoeuvre even as his eyes measured the distance between himself and the driver, noting the position of the steering wheel, gear-shift, clutch pedal, and foot-brake, storing up information for the moment when in three viciously decisive movements he would break the Frenchman's arm, silence the driver with a neck-chop, and hurl himself across the man's slumping body in a probably vain attempt to gain control of the wildly careering car. He leaned back in his seat, closing his eyes while his well-trained mind, sharpened and honed to a fine temper in Europe's most exacting school of espionage, the Ruritanian Agents' College, assessed his chances of survival when the limousine left the road. As it undoubtedly would, swerving across the path of other vehicles that would be powerless to stop and would smash into the high-sided truck with a rending and crumpling of metal, a shattering of glass, a desperate, devil's fanfare of horns drowning the screams of the limo's occupants as bones snapped, muscles were bloodily sliced, and flesh roasted with an evil, oily smell in the ensuing conflagration. It was a risk he had to take. He opened his eyes and saw, with a start, that the Frenchman was reaching into his pocket and speaking softly as he did so. Jonathan Doe leaned forward to catch the words, steeling himself for the action that must follow. The Frenchman said . . .

SHE:

. . . 'Perhaps madame would care for a chocolate?'

As he did, he drew from his pocket the largest box of chocolates Charley had ever seen, tastefully wrapped with an *élan* and a *panache* that positively screamed *Paris*. Though her every instinct counselled against it, her eyes were irresistibly drawn to a raspberry whirl. Her fingers trembling, she popped it into her mouth, thanking the stranger as she did so.

'It is very strange,' he said, his eyes dancing mockingly in his tanned, sardonic face, 'but I thought you would have taken a praline cracknell.'

'Why?' Charley burst out, wondering what he would say next.

He shrugged as only Frenchmen can shrug, with a rapid lifting and lowering of the shoulders. 'Who knows what a woman will choose?'

'Or a man?' Charley countered, suddenly resentful of his questioning.

'Je vous en prie,' he riposted, lapsing seriously into his native tongue, 'have a nougat ripple, they are – how do you say?' He frowned, struggling for the word that eluded him. 'Delicieux,' he said at last.

From under half-lowered lashes, Kathryne de Launay considered him. He might be amusing, this Frenchman. To fence with, to flirt with, even, perhaps . . . to love? Hastily she thrust from her mind the thought that challenged her total devotion to Jonathan.

'I think, monsieur,' she said, enunciating the words with devastating clarity, 'that you are trying to seduce me.'

His eyes blazing with anger or lust, she could not tell which, the Frenchman strained forward, almost pinning her to the seat, and hissed:

HE:

. . . 'Pardon, do you know which is the Space Needle?'

With considerable relief Jonathan Doe slipped back into his pocket his spring-loaded fountain pen. It would not be needed, after all, now that Frenchy had revealed himself as an operative of AA (*Agents Alliés*), an organization working in close collaboration with the RAC. Did the fool realize how close he had come to receiving a lethal intravenous injection of *encre*? Fortunately he had produced in the nick of time that coded reference to the Space Needle, the agreed signal for the first contact. Breathing more easily now, Jonathan Doe, *alias* Ivan Dubkovic, also known as the Camel, carefully uttered the pre-arranged reply:

'It is over there.'

'*Tiens*, it is of a formidable grandeur.' The European operative sounded impressed.

'The Americans know how to do things.' Jonathan Doe lolled negligently against the leatherette seat-back, seemingly at ease now, though his bantering manner belied the furious activity of a mind vitally engaged in reading the significance of every casual exchange. Already the Frenchman – a Provençal from the Camargue, estimated Dubkovic, whose own maternal grandmother hailed from that region – had told him much.

'It is not very old, perhaps?' The trench-coated man was speaking again.

'*Mais non*.' Jonathan Doe's tones were measured, his glance level. 'It was erected in 1962, when the World's Fair was held here in Seattle.'

The other nodded ruminatively. 'I have heard something of this.'

'After that highly successful event,' the Englishman continued calmly, 'the site remained in use, as the Seattle Center. Here you will find theatres, art galleries, concert halls, science exhibitions, a fun-fair' – he grimaced – 'and a veritable profusion of restaurants and cafés where you may sample the cuisine of America and Europe. Several buses stop at the Center, which can also be reached by monorail from Third Avenue Downtown.'

He paused, conscious of having said more than was strictly necessary.

'And the Needle?' The continental was nothing if not persistent.

'The Needle, as you see, is still there.'

'It is tall?' The other's inflection was questioning, uncertain.

In the recesses of Jonathan Doe's alert mind voices were urging prudence. He frowned. How much did the Frenchman really know, and how much should he, Ivan Dubkovic, the Camel, reveal?

'It is 605 feet high,' he slowly explained. Then, in impulsive response to the smile that suddenly illuminated the lean Gallic features of the man in the trench-coat, he added 'The observation deck and revolving restaurant offer 360-degree views of the city, Puget Sound, Lake Washington, and the Olympic Mountains.'

'Wonderful!' The grizzled veteran of a hundred sorties nodded slow appreciation. 'You have told me that which I needed to know.'

'*Bon!*' His business with the Frenchman done, Ivan Dubkovic's manner was suddenly brisk. Their paths would not cross again, and he recognized the wisdom of avoiding personal entanglements. 'Well, it's been . . .

SHE:

. . . a pleasant trip. Now why don't you all go inside and register, folks, and I'll be right along with your baggage.'

It seemed to Charley that the young driver with the romantic mop of dark curls reserved a special smile for her, and his eyes flickered an invitation to share unspeakable erotic delights. Sighing, she shrugged the impractical thought aside, and scuttled into the hotel in Jonathan's long-legged wake.

A prospect of almost sinful luxury greeted her amazed stare. The atrium of the Mogadon had obviously been designed with no restraining thought of expense, even in this land of untold wealth and sybaritic indulgence. In the centre of the building a huge fountain played, its silvery jets catching the iridescence of a myriad of concealed light bulbs. The water fell back into pools built at different levels and stocked with varieties of gorgeously coloured carp imported wholesale from Japan. Each pool was the centre of a space furnished with deep armchairs upholstered in the softest leather and occasional tables of genuine oak, curiously figured walnut, and richly glowing dark mahogany. Hangings and gathered drapes of velvet and other costly fabrics made enclosures of quiet intimacy hidden from prying eyes, hidden even from the eyes of those riding the glass elevators, banded in bronze, that ascended and descended amazingly through a simulated rainfall of shimmering glass rods and pendant lights. Seeing it all for the first time, Charley decided that it was absolutely indescribable.

Suddenly a gasp of disbelief assailed her throat, and she plunged forward, the carpet a deeply yielding hindrance to her every step, to where, by one of the pools, a solitary figure sat immersed in a book. She had recognized her friend and rival Serafina van Storm, the romantic novelist whose best-selling

triumphs concealed from the world the identity of Maisie Plunkett, head of the Geography Dept. Sensing Kathryne's approach,
Serafina raised her head, and then, amazed, rose gracefully to
her feet.

'Charley! Well, who would have thought it?'

Kathryne's full, sensual lips, their tempting outline discreetly
traced with a soft-toned lipstick, registered a faint *moue* of
amusement at her friend's deliberate affectation of the
vernacular.

'Maisie Plunkett,' she breezily countered, 'you're a sight for
sore eyes.'

And so she was. Surveying the svelte figure before her,
Kathryne could scarcely suppress the envious impulse to find
fault, but fault there was none to find. A sheath of glimmering
satin drew admiring eyes to the trim waist, the daring contour
of eager thighs, the firm breasts that needed no uplift from
cunningly-wired *soutien-gorge*. Serafina's silver-blonde hair was
swept back in classic severity from her pale oval face with its
exquisitely modelled features, the large hazel eyes that could
sometimes blur mistily and sometimes gleam with sharp intelligence, the small yet well-formed mouth with its row of even,
perfectly white teeth. A wide-brimmed smoke-grey felt hat that
would have looked out of place on any other woman only
lent a mischievous suggestion of wantonness to the flawless
composure of her face. She was wearing brown leather boots.
She was a picture.

'You staying here or what?' Kathryne enquired, cautiously,
hating her own intrusiveness. Still, with Serafina you never knew.
Barely six months previously she had broken up with Esteban,
and before that there had been Dimitri. Best to know at the
outset how the land lay, she reflected.

'In a place like this? That's a good one,' Serafina riposted,
languidly tossing her lovely head and setting in violent agitation
the diamond-encrusted gold pendants that hung from the tiny
pink ears men loved to nuzzle and bite. Her tenderly-modulated
voice took on a deeper, harsher tone, as she added, 'I'm with
Perce, aren't I? Staying at the Ace Motel and Diner we are, I
only come here to look at the lobby. and show myself off, just
in case.'

A tremor of genuine distress briefly ruffled the calm of
Kathryne's normally immaculate features.

'Hard luck, Maise,' she faltered, gulping back the sob that rose hotly into her throat. 'That's a real let-down, that is. Fancy coming all this way to put up at the Ace Motel and Diner! I should have a word with your travel agent if I were you.'

The glamorous writer shrugged.

'Mustn't grumble,' she softly intoned. 'It's better than teaching Geography.'

'Not half,' mused Kathryne de Launay. 'And after two weeks of this' – with jewel-bedecked fingers she gestured at their luxurious surroundings – 'don't expect me to enjoy coaching netball.'

Serafina's joyously tinkling laugh turned many heads.

'You staying a fortnight, then?' she enquired, decorum reclaiming her.

Kathryne frowned, and for a moment stood quietly immersed in thought.

'Not exactly,' she presently confessed. 'We're staying here . . .

HE:

. . . for twelve nights, I believe?'

Jonathan Doe's hand, poised to fill in the registration slip, was momentarily immobilized by incredulity. He had not expected that the second coded message would follow so quickly upon the first. He let a slow half-minute pass while he composed his thoughts, methodically smoothing from his features any trace of mental agitation. The eyes that he eventually raised to meet the bland gaze of the bald receptionist were coldly uncommunicative.

'I beg your pardon?' he asked, deliberately playing for time.

The receptionist sighed briefly, once, through his nose, and rephrased the question.

'Are you staying for twelve nights?'

There was no mistaking it this time. Ivan Dubkovic had been well-briefed. His masters had taught him to recognize the works of Shakespeare, an indispensable source of reference for any self-respecting RAC operative. More than that, he had been alerted to the possibility of an allusion to *Twelfth Night*, a copy of which was to be found in the pocket of Charley Doe's flight bag. Dubkovic had slipped it there himself, on the pretext of giving her an opportunity to work on next year's A-level set book.

'Twelve nights, yes.'

'Fill in the card, please.'

The hand that swivelled the pad on which the registration card lay was perfectly steady. This was no greenhorn, in the field for the first time. Dubkovic observed with professional interest the stiff white collar and the boldly-knotted yet tastefully-chosen gray tie – the one, he knew, concealing a flexible blade of blue steel, delicate yet capable of disembowelling an opponent in hand-to-hand fighting, the other completely camouflaging the garrotting wire issued as standard equipment to operatives in all the major intelligence agencies. Ivan Dubkovic felt the desk clerk's eyes raking him as he carefully inscribed the United Kingdom postcode invented for him by the RAC. They were lazy eyes, almost black, with touches of green in the iris, but their indolence was belied by the stark energy of the musculature above the bridge of the nose, a sure token of concentrated power.

Doe completed his task, a nerve twitching gently in his left cheek. 'There you are,' he said.

'Thank you,' said the bald man, significantly. 'The bell captain will take care of your baggage.'

His every nerve shrilling a strident warning, Jonathan Doe hurled himself across the lobby, caroming off several guests and reaching Charley just in time to. . .

HE:

. . . tear her rudely away from her friend and propel her towards the waiting elevator. Resentment seared her system as, blinking back her tears, she fled through the open doors. How could Jonathan treat her like this? Did he think she was – her mind fought blindly, desperately, with the vocabulary that threatened to elude her – ugly? Only the bell captain's frankly appraising glance restored her wilting self-regard, telling her that she was desirable, that her nose was firm and straight and her breasts were pointed. Her eyes were a question that drew from him an unspoken challenge, a blatant, shameless invitation to which she could only return a tremulous and utterly silent assent.

'Tenth floor,' he said, his back tapering vigorously to firm loins.

As the elevator rapidly rose, Kathryne gazed idly down through its encircling glass, her sophisticated mind registering and rejecting the all-too-familiar vistas of soulless luxury. One day, she told herself, she would be free of all this, free to wander barefoot through the fields and wear outsize tartan shirts over simply faded blue jeans. Jonathan would give up his life as a spy and a famous University Lecturer, and they would keep chickens. And then . . . And then . . .

HE:

. . . and then it happened. Between the eighth and the ninth floors the elevator jerked to a halt.

Jonathan Doe's brain, working with a precision and speed beyond the scope of the most advanced computer, told him exactly what had occurred. The elevator had broken down. Far below, he could imagine the anger that would presently grow to alarm, the alarm that would kindle to panic, swirling in a fiery vortex round the lobby, leaving no one untouched by the scorching wind of terror. He hoped someone had gone to tell the bald man. The bell captain, Dubkovic could see, would be useless, incapable of doing what might have to be done when the time came to do it. It would be left to the Camel to open the suitcase with the coded lock and find, as the air in the elevator grew chokingly dense with carbon dioxide, the multi-tool that would remove the back panels and the rope-soled sandals that would enable the party to attempt, one at a time, the perilous ascent of the dark, narrow shaft, up cables that human beings were never intended to climb. His gorge rose at the thought, but the Camel's icy assurance insisted that it could be done. Jonathan Doe's restless eyes took shrewd cognizance of the fact that Charley was wearing a skirt. That would only get in the way when it came to climbing the cables. It would have to come off. He was on the point of communicating his decision when. . .

SHE:

. . . the elevator resumed its progress, somewhat to the relief of Charley, who felt her heart fluttering at the thrilling nearness of the bell captain's taut, athletic frame and flat stomach. Soon they were being shown into a spacious and airy apartment, bounded on one side by a large window and balcony, and on the other three sides by large walls decorated with impeccable taste. While Charley threw herself down on the large expensive bed, Jonathan . . .

HE:

. . . picked up the phone and dialled room service. For him a beefburger on rye bread with onion rings and French fries, but kill the ketchup, and a Michelob, and for the broad, what the hell, a short stack of pancakes and a Shirley Temple. And coffee, hot and strong. Afterwards there would be time . . .

SHE:

. . . to unpack, she told him. But already she had found, in her flight bag, the copy of *Twelfth Night* he had discovered on the bookstall – *the* bookstall – *their* bookstall – and had had bound in expensive calf leather for her birthday. Her heart went out to him in fluttering tenderness as he sat down beside her and took his shoes off. She opened the book at a venture.

'What country, friends, is this?' she read, in a clear, girlish voice modulated by the impeccably British tones of Kathryne de Launay.

Jonathan Doe, alias Ivan Dubkovic, a.k.a. the Camel, grinned drowsily.

'This is America, kid,' he said, and his arms reached out for her.

They did not answer when the waiter tapped at the door. They were both fast asleep, dreaming of the future that would always be theirs.

References and bibliographical note

Quotations from the following magazine stories and novels have appeared in this essay.

Stories

[Anonymous] 'Too Much Love', *True Story*, April 1987
Helen Lesley Beaton, 'Dark Designs', *Woman's Weekly*, 12 November 1983
Maeve Binchy, 'Change of Heart', *Woman*, 17 December 1983
Colleen Bridgnell, 'Man in the Middle', *My Weekly*, 1 March 1986
Helen Forrester, 'A Matter of Friendship', *Woman*, 22 November 1986
Sue Gee, 'Someone Remembered', *Woman*, 17 December 1983
Michelle Lee, 'Travelling Lady', *My Weekly*, 1 March 1987
Levanah Lloyd, 'House of Whispers' (serial), *My Weekly*, 1 March 1986
P. E. M. Nesbitt, 'Watch It, Mrs Ingram!', *My Weekly*, 1 March 1986
Barbara Perkins, 'Marina's Sister' (serial), *Woman's Weekly*, 12 November 1983
Margaret Redfern, 'Dark Rhapsody' (serial), *Woman's Weekly*, 28 March 1987
Amanda Sayle, 'The Last Frontier' (serial), *Woman's Own*, 10 January 1987
Kathryn Stacey, 'The Governess' (serial), *Woman's Weekly*, 28 March 1987
Anne Weal, 'Summer's Awakening' (serial), *Woman's Weekly*, 12 November 1983

(For numerous incidental illustrations – word-items, phrases – I am further indebted to stories in *Annabelle*, *My Story*, *My Weekly*, *True Romances*, *True Story*, *Woman*, *Woman's Own*, *Woman's Realm*, and *Woman's Weekly*.)

Novels: romances and thrillers

Desmond Bagley, *Night of Error* (1984) Collins, London
Barbara Cartland, *The Naked Battle* (1978) Arrow Books, London, repr. 1982

Raymond Chandler, *Farewell, My Lovely* (1940) Penguin, London, repr. 1986

James Clavell, *King Rat* (1962) Coronet Books, London, repr. 1982

Catherine Cookson, *Tilly Trotter* (1980) Corgi, London, repr. 1981

Alfred Coppel, *34 East* (1974) Pan Books, London, repr. 1976

Ian Fleming, *Live and Let Die* (1954) Pan Books, London, repr. 1973

Ian Fleming, *Diamonds are Forever* (1956) Pan Books, London, repr. 1965

Frederick Forsyth, *The Day of the Jackal* (1971) Corgi, London, repr. 1987

Frederick Forsyth, *The Devil's Alternative* (1979) Corgi, London, repr. 1983

Paul Gallico, *The Poseidon Adventure* (1974) Pan Books, London, repr. 1975

John Gardner, *License Renewed* (1981) Berkley Books, New York, repr. 1982

Victoria Holt, *Mistress of Mellyn* (1971) Fontana Books, London, repr. 1976

Hammond Innes, *Levkas Man* (1971) Fontana Books, London, repr. 1973

Claudia Jameson, *Escape to Love* (1981) Mills and Boon, London, repr. 1982

Judith Krantz, *Mistral's Daughter* (1983) Corgi, London, repr. 1984

Robert Ludlum, *The Parsifal Mosaic* (1982) Bantam Books, New York, repr. 1983

Simon Raven, *The Survivors* (1976) Panther Books, London, repr. 1985

Wilbur Smith, *Eagle in the Sky* (1974) Pan Books, London, repr. 1975

Wilbur Smith, *The Leopard Hunts in Darkness* (1984) Guild Publishing, London

Jacqueline Susann, *Valley of the Dolls* (1966) Corgi, London, repr. 1977

Anne Weal, *Bed of Roses* (1981) Mills and Boon, London

Other references

Jane Austen, *Northanger Abbey*; Joseph Conrad, *A Smile of Fortune*; Stella Gibbons, *Cold Comfort Farm* (1932) Penguin Books, London, repr. 1987; Thomas Hardy, *The Mayor of Casterbridge*; Ernest Hemingway, *The Short Happy Life of Francis Macomber* and *The Snows of Kilimanjaro*; D. H. Lawrence, *The Fox*.

Bibliographical note

There is much current interest in the sociology and ideology of modern popular fiction, and in the literary theory of certain genres, notably Science Fiction and 'Utopian' writing; there appears, however, to be very little of substance on questions of style. A good general orientation is provided by Christopher Pawling (ed.), *Popular Fiction and Social Change* (Macmillan, London, 1984, repr. 1985). This is a collection of essays by university and polytechnic teachers working in the fields of Sociology or Communication Studies. It has a very useful annotated bibliography. Other general books are C. W. Bigsby (ed.), *Approaches to Popular Culture* (Edward Arnold, London, 1976; a symposium with essays by literary critics, social historians, and linguists) and S. Hall and P. Whannel, *The Popular Arts* (Hutchinson, London, 1964). A survey of British and American popular novels of a recent decade is made by J. Sutherland, *Bestsellers: Popular Fiction of the 1970s* (RKP, London, 1981). R. Anderson, *The Purple Heart-Throbs* (Hodder and Stoughton, London, 1974) studies the growth of popular romantic fiction; J. King and M. Stott (eds), *Is This Your Life?* (Virago, London, 1977) contains essays criticizing the images of women presented in fiction, in films, and on television. A more recent book with chapters on His and Hers is J. Batsleer, T. Davies, R. O'Rourke and C. Weedon, *Rewriting English: Cultural Politics of Gender and Class* (Methuen, London, 1985). On the spy thriller and the hero as secret agent, there are recent publications by T. Bennett and J. Woollacott, *Bond and Beyond: The Political Career of a Popular Hero* (Macmillan, London, 1986), and M. Denning, *Cover Stories: Narrative and Ideology in the British Spy Thriller* (Routledge, London, 1988). With reference to the Bond stories and the implications of that kind of narrative, one should mention Umberto Eco, *The Role of the Reader: Explorations in the Semiotics of Texts* (Indiana University Press, Bloomington, 1978).

Index